USDA

United States
Department of
Agriculture

Forest
Service

Northern
Research Station

General Technical
Report NRS-29

Woody Detritus Density and Density Reduction Factors for Tree Species in the United States: A Synthesis

Mark E. Harmon, Christopher W. Woodall, Becky Fasth, and Jay Sexton

Abstract

Woody detritus biomass estimates are most often achieved by determining the volume of dead wood and then converting to mass by use of density values. There have been few studies on how density (mass/volume) of this material changes during the decay process. The goal of this study was to synthesize both published and unpublished data on woody detritus density so as to improve estimates of coarse woody detritus (CWD) and fine woody detritus (FWD) biomass across the diverse forests of the United States. In the case of CWD, a total of 88 species were found to have data on densities for five decay classes that had been published and/or collected in North America from the boreal to the tropical zones. In general, density declined from decay class 1 to 5 with at least five density reduction patterns observed. For FWD, our search indicated approximately 25 species had been sampled. FWD density was a function of piece diameter and the general state of decay. We determined that by sampling representative species within a genus, the uncertainty of CWD estimates could be reduced by up to 50 percent over not having sampled a genus. Our analysis indicated that the uncertainty of FWD mass estimation ranged from 12 to 19 percent when FWD relative density was estimated. We conclude that a more systematic sampling of CWD and FWD density is needed for major species if uncertainties of mass estimates nationwide are to be reduced.

The Authors

MARK E. HARMON, Richardson Chair and Professor, Department of Forest Science, Oregon State University

CHRISTOPHER W. WOODALL, Research Forester, U.S. Forest Service, Northern Research Station

BECKY FASTH, Research Assistant, Department of Forest Science, Oregon State University

JAY SEXTON, Senior Research Assistant, Department of Forest Science, Oregon State University

CONTENTS

(Contents continued on next page)

CONTENTS (continued)

INTRODUCTION

IMPORTANCE OF WOODY DETRITUS

Woody detritus or dead wood is an important part of forest ecosystems. Although woody detritus is associated with many ecological benefits (plant and animal habitat, carbon, nutrient and water storage, as well as soil formation), the magnitude of these benefits varies with the species of log, the environment (i.e., climate, soil characteristics, topography), and the amount of dead wood on a site (Franklin et al. 1987, Harmon et al. 1986, Triska and Cromack 1980). The same is true for possible negative aspects of this material such as a source of fuel influencing fire behavior and smoke emissions. Therefore, this material is increasingly being included in ecological studies and environmental assessments, and the number of publications on this subject is rapidly growing.

Woody detritus takes many forms. It may range from sound to highly decayed materials. Woody detritus is present as roots, stumps, branches (including attached dead branches), standing dead (i.e., snags), downed material, and buried wood in litter, duff, and mineral soil. Very few inventories measure all these forms and size classes—snags and downed material being the most commonly measured. For example, the Forest Inventory and Analysis (FIA) program of the U.S. Forest Service conducts a national inventory of woody material including standing dead, FWD (fine woody detritus), and CWD (coarse woody detritus) (for more details, see Woodall and Monleon 2008). FWD with the exception of roots is typically less than 7.6 to 10 cm, the former size limit being based on lag-times of fuels (i.e., the time to equilibrate with the atmosphere in terms of moisture content; see Burgan 1988). For woody roots the size break is usually 2 mm, which is based on conventions on the maximum size of live fine roots. CWD exceeds these diameters but also typically must exceed a length of 1 m. It can either be standing (e.g., snags) or downed (e.g., logs).

MEASUREMENT OF WOODY DETRITUS

Measurements of woody detritus abundance include the number of pieces per area, volume, mass, and cover (typically either basal area for snags or projected cover for logs). Many ecosystem functions, such as a fuel for fire, depend on mass. However, there is a basic problem because the mass of woody detritus is not easy to directly measure unless the material is very small. Volume is easier to measure, and most methods, be they transect- or plot-based, measure piece dimensions to estimate volume (Brown 1974, Harmon and Sexton 1996). Mass can be derived from volume if the density (i.e., mass/volume) of this material is known. A similar problem exists with live trees because these are also rarely weighed directly. Rather, equations to predict volume from more easily measured dimensions such as diameter at breast height and/or height are established. Volume can then be converted to mass using the density of wood and bark. Unfortunately, estimation of woody detritus amounts is not as straightforward as for live trees. Woody detritus is often irregular in shape relative to live trees and therefore volume is estimated directly for each piece by techniques such as line intercepts or dimensional measures in plots. Moreover, rather than a single density value per species, the density of woody detritus pieces also depends on the extent of decomposition. This change can be dealt with by recognizing various decay classes of material and determining the density of each decay class. When decay class-specific density and elemental concentrations are coupled with the volume in each decay class, one can estimate the mass, carbon, and nutrient stores of woody detritus.

The downed woody material (DWM) sampling design of the FIA program uses line-intersect transects to estimate the volume of downed CWD and FWD, but not their biomass (Woodall and Williams 2005). Biomass conversion constants published in the literature are currently used to convert volume to biomass. Two constants are used: (1) the initial density (i.e., specific gravity) and (2) a decay reduction factor that accounts for the decline in density as this form of detritus decomposes. Unfortunately, there are very few published values of the decay class-specific density or decay reduction factors; these have typically been available only for a few western tree species (Sollins et al. 1987). The little work that has been done has shown that species have different patterns of density decline (Yatskov et al. 1993). Thus, uncertainty in biomass estimates can be introduced if the incorrect pattern is assumed for a species that has not been studied. FIA's own simulation studies have shown that a 15-percent variation in biomass conversion constants could affect a plot's total DWM biomass estimate by 5 percent (Woodall and Lutes 2004). However, because FIA uses decay reduction factors based on a few western tree species for the entire Nation, conversion constants may vary in excess of 50 percent causing substantial error in biomass estimates.

OBJECTIVES

Given the fact woody detritus inventories are rapidly becoming a common component of forest resource inventories around the world, there is great need to refine the constants used in biomass estimation procedures for both CWD and FWD. While the current datasets on changes in wood density with decomposition are far from ideal, a substantial amount of published and unpublished data exists. Therefore, the goal of this study was to synthesize both published and unpublished data on woody detritus density and carbon content to improve estimates of CWD and FWD biomass and carbon across the diverse forests of the United States. The specific objectives of this study are to (1) estimate CWD and FWD density across decay classes for the tree species currently considered by the FIA inventory, (2) develop a methodology to estimate the uncertainty in these estimates, (3) provide examples of how these estimates can be used, (4) suggest future study directions to reduce uncertainty in these estimates, and (5) provide preliminary biomass to carbon conversion factors.

DATA, METHODS, AND ANALYSIS

DATA

We assembled data from two sources. Over the years a substantial quantity of decayed wood density data has been generated by the Andrews Long-term Ecological Research (LTER) program. Some of this data has been published, but much of it has not, at least in terms of densities for decay classes. This program has also produced a large dataset on undecayed branch density as part of branch decomposition studies that have been conducted over the years. The other source was the published literature, which, although not as extensive as the first source, does provide information for many systems not sampled (Appendix 1).

FIELD METHODS COMMON TO MOST STUDIES
Steps in Estimating Dead Wood Mass

Estimating the mass of decomposing wood involves several steps. Ideally one would weigh the mass of woody debris in an area, but realistically this would be time consuming and physically difficult. The first step is to measure the density of the wood to be inventoried by sampling wood and bark in a range of decay states. The second step is to determine the volume of the woody detritus in the inventory area by decay classes. The third step is to convert the volume to mass using the decay class-specific density values. Finally, total mass can be converted to specific elemental stores by knowing the concentration of elements such as carbon and nitrogen. Unfortunately, volume inventories are often conducted without knowledge of how density or nutrient contents change with decay class. While some substitution of these conversion factors is inevitable, it has been common to use western U.S. conifer values for many temperate biomes and in some cases tropical ones. This introduces substantial uncertainty in woody detritus mass and other related estimates (e.g., carbon stocks, fuel loadings, smoke emissions).

Assessing the State of Decay of Woody Detritus

Decay classes are a subjective way to break the decomposition process, which is a continuum, into recognizable stages. While continuous methods using techniques such as ordination exist (Harmon et al. 1987), they are very awkward to implement in the field. Classes can be defined by the presence of criteria that tend to be associated with certain decay classes. However, there can be a great deal of variation within and between pieces of decomposing wood, and this may cause misclassification of some individuals. By averaging over a large number of pieces, these errors tend to cancel out.

The number of decay classes used varies from study to study. For CWD, as many as 13 classes and as few as 2 classes have been used in the past (Harmon et al. 1986). One of the more common systems developed in the Pacific Northwest uses five decay classes (Sollins 1982). For FWD, a single average number is often used, although a separation into undecayed or fresh versus decayed has also been used especially after recent disturbance (Brown 1974). The density of decayed FWD tends to be highly variable, and it is highly dependent on whether pieces are added in a pulse or continuously. When added as a pulse, many FWD pieces have similar densities that decrease through time. When continuously added, the average density of FWD is likely to be fairly consistent; however, there is a great range in densities depending on when a particular piece was added.

It has been demonstrated that wood density generally declines as decay advances with some exceptions. For CWD, some species have very decay resistant heartwood (e.g., black locust, *Robinia pseudoacacia*). If the outer decayed sapwood and bark layers disappear via respiration or fragmentation and the residual heartwood has little decay, then more advanced decay classes can theoretically have an increase in density. The same can be true for FWD such as branches, which often lose decomposed outer wood as decomposition proceeds. This often results in an undecayed, resin-impregnated core of wood being left; as the proportion of this resin-impregnated wood increases the density can increase.

Density Determination

Density is expressed as a dry mass divided by green volume in most cases, although density can be determined in alternative ways. For example, recently resistance drill systems have been used, although these are usually calibrated to traditional methods. For FWD it is typical to collect a random sample within an area or along transects. For CWD a number of logs, snags, or stumps of each decay class are located and then subsampled with a chainsaw to remove cross-sections along the stem. Alternatively, a coring device is used to remove samples, although this can be used only for relatively sound wood. Key characteristics such as presence of leaves, twigs, branches, bark, cross-sectional shape, wood hardness, and strength are typically recorded. Volume is determined either by displacement in water or a particulate solid (e.g., millet seed), taking a known volume using a core, or by measuring external dimensions. While determining volume using water displacement is probably the most accurate method for solid samples, it is relatively slow and works best for small volumes. However, it is very difficult to use this method for highly decomposed wood and bark, which means either decay classes with this material are not included or only the more solid pieces are examined leading to an uncertainty or outright bias for more advanced stages of decay. Coring suffers from the same problem regarding the extent of decay present. While volumes determined by external dimensions are less precise, these measurements can be taken quite rapidly in the field on very large volumes. This eliminates bias and leads to a better averaging of density within a piece.

Mass Determination

Mass of samples is typically determined by drying in an oven, often at temperatures ranging between 55 and 75 °C until mass remains constant. This can take weeks for even small cross-sections. To speed up drying times, smaller subsamples are often used. This entails weighing the entire sample and then subsampling for moisture determination. The ratio of oven dried mass to the fresh mass of the subsample is used to convert the fresh mass to dry mass of the entire sample.

As noted above, for FWD, decay classes are not usually noted, although green versus decayed material generally may be recorded separately. Subsamples are sometimes taken to determine density for a particular ecosystem, but this is rarely done and the default values presented in Brown (1974) are often used. When sampled, volume is determined by measuring dimensions of pieces or by volume displacement. Mass is determined via oven drying using approaches similar to that of CWD.

ANALYSIS

Woody detritus density was expressed in two ways: absolute density (mass/green volume) and relative density (decayed density/undecayed density). Relative density is alternatively called the density reduction factor in the FIA system. We used the existing data to estimate both variables for all the species inventoried by the FIA. In addition to estimating the mean values, we estimated the uncertainty associated with these estimates of density, with the least uncertainty for species that had been sampled and the most for genera that had not been sampled. To estimate densities for species that had not been sampled, we examined the pattern of density reduction for related species and genera that had been sampled. In the case of CWD, we compared absolute and relative density among five decay classes. For FWD, we were able to use only two decay classes (i.e., undecayed versus decayed), although we did this for three size classes.

Data Processing

When several sources of data for a species, genus, decay class, or size class were available, we combined the values to estimate an average and standard error. When sample sizes were listed, we used those to weight the average as well as the standard error of the samples. When sample sizes were not listed, we calculated a simple average and used the highest observed standard error as an estimate of uncertainty. For undecayed wood density of CWD, we used estimates provided by the FIA database, which is largely derived from the Wood Handbook (U.S. Department of Agriculture 1999). Although not all FWD studies reported species-specific values, we assumed that they represented the values of the dominant species in the ecosystem from which they had been sampled.

CWD Predictions

We used the available information to estimate the CWD density (absolute and relative) of each species currently encountered in the national FIA inventory. While it is important to estimate the mean density of decayed wood for all species, it is even more important to estimate the uncertainty introduced in this process. We devised a system in which the uncertainty would increase as the degree of extrapolation increased. Minimal extrapolation was involved when a species had been sampled and maximum extrapolation was involved when a genus had not been sampled. The uncertainty was expressed as the standard error of the mean. There were three levels of uncertainty:

A. Species that had been sampled. In this case the mean was the average of all the observed values and the uncertainty was represented by the standard error of the mean. The uncertainty in relative density was calculated as the standard error of the mean absolute density divided by the undecayed density. In this case the uncertainty term only involved sampling error.

B. Genera that had been sampled. If a species had not been sampled, but others in its genus had been sampled then there was some question as to where the mean would lie. The mean density was estimated by averaging the minimum and maximum relative density for the species in the genus that had been sampled. The absolute density was determined by multiplying the undecayed density of that species by the mean relative density. In this case the uncertainty involved not only sampling error, but also uncertainty about the mean itself. We used the maximum difference of mean relative density observed in the genus for each decay class to provide an estimate of uncertainty associated with the genus mean. This was then increased by two standard errors of the mean of the relative density for observed species to account for sampling errors. We then assumed that 95 percent of the estimates of the mean would fall within that range and divided it by 4 to rescale it to something akin to a standard error. The uncertainty of the absolute density was then calculated by multiplying the undecayed density of the species by the uncertainty in the relative density.

C. Species and genus not sampled. In this case the mean could lie anywhere between the minimum and maximum of the observed values. We therefore estimated the mean as the average of the minimum and maximum observed values of relative density. The absolute density was the product of the mean relative density and the undecayed density. The uncertainty was calculated as when only genera were sampled (section B above); however, we used the maximum difference in relative density means of all the species that had been examined.

FWD Predictions

We also estimated green and decayed density of FWD of the species encountered in the FIA inventory. For undecayed density, we used actual measures or in most cases derived this from undecayed branch density to undecayed bole density ratios (branch to bole ratios). For decayed density, we used either means of observed values or derived them from decayed versus undecayed FWD density ratios. As with CWD, in addition to estimating the mean value, we also estimated the uncertainty in FWD estimates based on the level of information available:

A. Species that had been sampled for FWD density. We used the mean and standard error of the observed values of undecayed and decayed density. We calculated the relative density by dividing the mean by the undecayed density. We calculated the uncertainty of the relative density by dividing the standard error of decayed density by the mean undecayed density. When the standard error had not been reported for a species, we multiplied the maximum relative variation of species where this statistic had been reported by the mean density of the species in question to provide some estimate of uncertainty.

B. Species lacking undecayed FWD density values. We used the mean bole density multiplied by the mean ratio of branch to bole density to estimate undecayed FWD density. The uncertainty in undecayed FWD density using this method was determined by multiplying the standard error of this ratio for all species with observations by the bole density of the species that was being estimated.

C. Species lacking decayed FWD density. Estimates of decayed FWD density for species that have not been sampled were computed from the product of the mean ratio of decayed to green branch density for species and the green density of the species to be estimated. The uncertainty in the decayed FWD density for this set of species was estimated by:

$$U_{Decayed\ FWD} = sqrt\ (ID^2*U_{ID}^2 + DGR^2*U_{DGR}^2)$$

where $U_{Decayed\ FWD}$ is the uncertainty in decayed FWD density, ID is the mean initial density, U_{ID} is the uncertainty in initial density, DGR is the decay to undecayed ratio, and U_{DGR} is the uncertainty in the undecayed ratio. This formula accounts for the fact that uncertainty for decayed FWD density is a function of two uncertainties. Our formula assumed no correlation between the uncertainties.

Analysis of Uncertainty on CWD Mass Estimates

We analyzed the uncertainty of CWD mass estimates caused by using current knowledge about relative density of decay classes. This was achieved by applying various density reduction patterns that are commonly observed to the following likely decay class volume distributions:

A. Normal distribution. The distribution of decay classes with respect to volume depends on the time interval that the decay class represents as well as the nature of the inputs. For the five decay class system we used, the tendency is for the time interval represented to increase geometrically as decay classes advance. For example, decay class 2 lasts about twice as long as decay class 1, and decay class 3 lasts roughly twice as long as decay class 2, etc. If the input of dead trees to the forest is uniform over time, this tends to result in a peaked volume distribution. Decay class 3 has the most volume because it includes a relatively long period relative to decay classes 1 and 2 and has not lost a great deal of volume to decomposition relative to decay classes 4 and 5. A steady input of CWD, therefore, leads to a normal distribution of decay classes in terms of volume (Harmon et al. 1986).

B. Exponential distributions. If there is a pulse in dead tree inputs, one can also have a peak in volume that advances from decay class to decay class as the forest ages. To assess a situation in which there had been a recent pulse of input, we used a negative exponential volume distribution. To look at a pulse that occurred in the distant past, we used the complement of this distribution (i.e., classes 1 and 5 were switched, etc).

C. Uniform distribution. Although not common, a uniform distribution was used where the volume of each decay class was equal to determine an "average" uncertainty.

D. Observed distribution. This was based on large-scale summaries from the FIA databases for Maine and gives a sense of the actual operational uncertainty likely to be encountered. The data were taken from 200 plots and involved approximately 2,400 CWD pieces.

To calculate the uncertainty in CWD biomass estimates, the relative volume in each decay class was multiplied by a range of relative density reduction patterns to assess the range of mass estimates that would occur. The relative density reduction patterns that were investigated included (1) a steady decrease from decay class to decay class, (2) an asymptotic pattern with decay classes 4 and 5 similar, (3) a mid-plateau in density decline with decay classes 2 and 3 being similar, and (4) the pattern for Douglas-fir (the most commonly used pattern in previous studies). We also assessed the uncertainty for a well-sampled species (Douglas-fir) and a well-sampled genus (pines) as well as the minimum and maximum relative values observed. The latter two patterns place upper and lower uncertainty bounds on species or genera that have not been sampled. For most cases, the products of relative volume and relative density for each decay class for each relative density reduction pattern were summed and then compared to the value for Douglas-fir, which serves as a useful reference given that this pattern of density change has been used frequently. The exception was that for the overall minimum and maximum relative densities we used the mean of all species as the reference.

Analysis of Uncertainty on FWD Mass Estimates

We assessed the importance of two facets of uncertainty for estimates of FWD mass. The first aspect was the effect of having directly determined the relative density of decayed FWD; this was assessed by comparing the uncertainty in relative density of species that had actual samples versus those that did not. The second aspect involved the fact that the current system estimates an average FWD relative density, but does not account for the effect of pulses of input. Given that many sound branches and tops are left after disturbances such as harvests, pulses of FWD input are common. Immediately after a disturbance, FWD density is likely to be close to the undecayed density. As the time since the disturbance increases, the overall density of FWD is likely to decline at least until new material replaces it. To mimic this situation, we tracked the abundance and relative density of two sources of wood: a pulse and that due to regular mortality processes. For the pulse, we assumed the abundance of this FWD pool would follow a negative exponential decline. We assumed the density of the pulse would also decline, but that density would asymptote to reflect the presence of decay resistant portions of branches (i.e., knots). For the FWD generated by regular mortality processes, we assumed that pool would gradually accumulate and that the density would decline to a lesser degree given that undecayed wood is being added regularly. This asymptote was assumed to equal the average value we found in our analysis of the FWD dataset. We assumed the rate the pulse FWD was lost was the same as the rate the new FWD accumulated. Given that the accumulation rate is often close to the disappearance rate, this assumption is reasonable (Olson 1963). We explored the effect of not knowing the decay state of FWD by varying the size of the pulse from 5, 10, and 20 times the size of the regular FWD pool. We also varied the asymptotic density of the pulse of FWD from a relative density of 0.1 to 0.4 as well as explored the effect of the decomposition rate of FWD. We then noted the difference between the minimum and the average relative density because this indicated the uncertainty that might be introduced by not noting the decay state of FWD.

Biomass to Carbon Conversion Factors

We reviewed the literature to find estimates of the carbon concentration of dead wood in various states of decomposition. Given the paucity of data, we averaged across all species within CWD decay classes to derive a mean estimate. For FWD we averaged across all species for undecayed and decayed wood. We used all available data to derive a standard error of carbon concentration, weighting these estimates by the sample sizes reported in the publications.

RESULTS

QUALITATIVE CHANGES IN CWD DECAY CLASSES

The following describes the general qualitative changes observed as logs decompose. While not all species move through this exact progression, many do; major exceptions are noted. Decay class 1 logs are the least decomposed, with most having leaves still attached and all having intact bark, fine twigs, and branches. Logs originating from cutting may not have branches and twigs, but the cuts appear fresh and have not yet turned gray due to sun bleaching. Decay class 2 logs are ones starting to decompose, leaves largely are absent, and many of the fine twigs have fallen off the larger branches. Bark is typically loose, but only starting to fall off the log. An exception would be for the genera *Betula* and *Prunus*, which tend to retain bark throughout decomposition. For all species, there is evidence the surface layers of the wood are decomposing, but the inner, central region of the wood is undecayed unless previously infected with heart rots. For logs originating from cutting, the ends are gray from sun bleaching. Decay class 3 logs have only a few large branches remaining, often in the form of stubs, the bark is falling off in large patches, and evidence of sloughing of sapwood is also evident. The outer wood is easily crushed by hand, although the inner portions can appear completely sound. Despite the large amount of decay, decay class 3 logs are able to support their own weight along most of their length. For certain genera with decay resistant heartwoods, such as *Calocedrus*, *Quercus*, and *Thuja*, decayed sapwood may fall off to the extent that relatively sound heartwood may form the outer surface. Decay class 4 logs cannot support their own weight and most of their length conforms to the contours of the underlying ground. Although circular cross-sections can remain, much of the log forms an elliptical cross-section. Branches, if present, are short stubs, which move when pulled. This indicates decay has spread to the innermost portions of the log and has weakened the wood considerably. Bark, if present, is in small loose patches on the log and found in piles alongside or under the log. In the case of the genera *Betula* and *Prunus*, the bark loosely surrounds the inner, highly decomposed wood. Decay class 5 logs are the most decomposed, of elliptical shape (the long axis is often many times that of the short axis), and are beginning to be incorporated into the forest floor. The wood is extremely decayed, usually in the form of cubical brown rot that can be easily crushed by hand. Bark is not evident from the surface (except for the genera *Betula* and *Prunus*) and in most cases underlies the extremely decomposed wood.

DENSITY OF DECOMPOSING CWD

A total of 88 species were found to have data on CWD decay class densities that had been published and/or collected from North America from the boreal to the tropical zones. Most species (53) were from either boreal or temperate ecosystems. A total of 49 genera had some data about CWD decay class density, most of which were represented by one species. Of the species compiled, 60 were hardwood and 28 were softwood species.

Examining all the species that have been sampled reveals that wood density of CWD decay classes declines as expected, but that it is highly variable (Fig. 1). Much of this variation is associated with variation in the initial density, which ranges from 0.25 to 0.95 g/cm³. Expressed as a percent, minimum and maximum initial densities are 52 percent lower and 95 percent higher than the mean value, respectively. The relative variation appears to increase through decay class 3 and then declines for decay classes 4 and 5. This pattern may be caused by decomposition and wood's lack of structural integrity below a certain density.

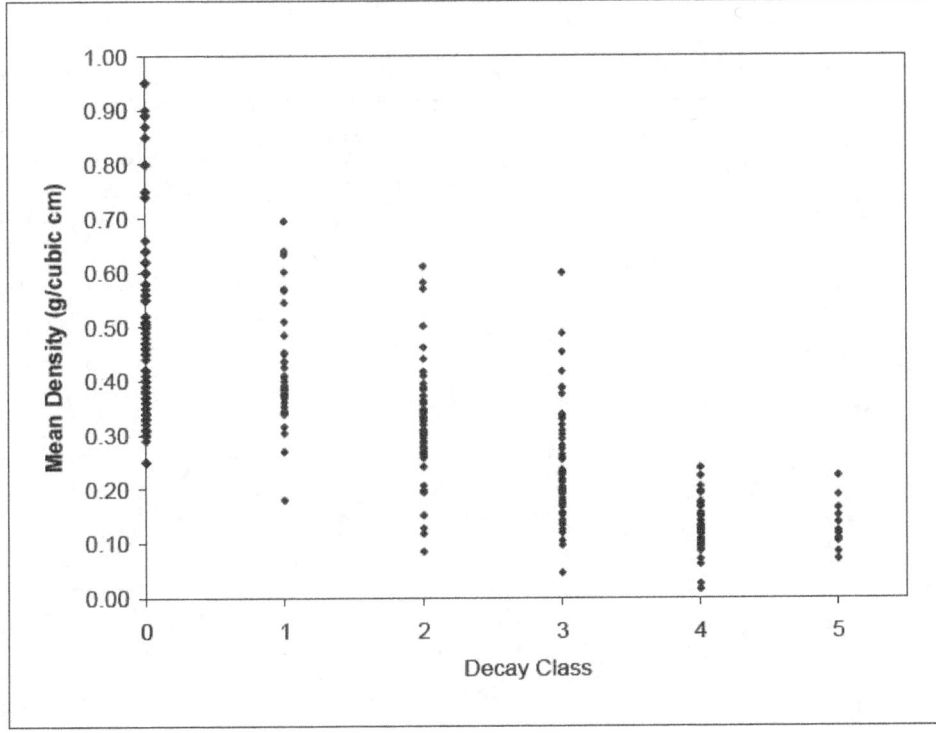

Figure 1.—Density of all species sampled by decay class. Each point represents the mean of a species that has been sampled for each decay class.

Comparison of hardwood and softwood mean density indicates that softwoods have a slightly lower density than hardwoods for decay classes 1 to 3 (Fig. 2). However, the mean densities of decay class 4 are quite similar for softwoods and hardwoods. Hardwood density, at least for undecayed wood and decay classes 1 to 3, appears more variable than softwood density. The variation, expressed as a range, within these groups is much higher than the variation between these two groups. This classification would therefore not seem to be a useful way to stratify unsampled species, although the uncertainty for softwood density is considerably lower than that for hardwoods.

CWD DENSITY REDUCTION PATTERNS

When all species that have been sampled are considered, there is a clear decrease in relative density as CWD decay class advances (Fig. 3). Although the mean relative density exhibits a steady decline, the maximum and minimum relative density can be as much as 60 percent higher or 40 percent lower than the mean, respectively. The greatest differences between the minimum and maximum appear in decay classes 2 and 3, but even for decay class 1 there is considerable variation. Despite the high level of variation observed, relative density is less variable than absolute density. This indicates that removing the effect of initial density can help reduce uncertainty when estimating density of unsampled species.

As with absolute density, dividing the species into hardwoods and softwoods does not appear to help reduce uncertainty in estimating relative density.

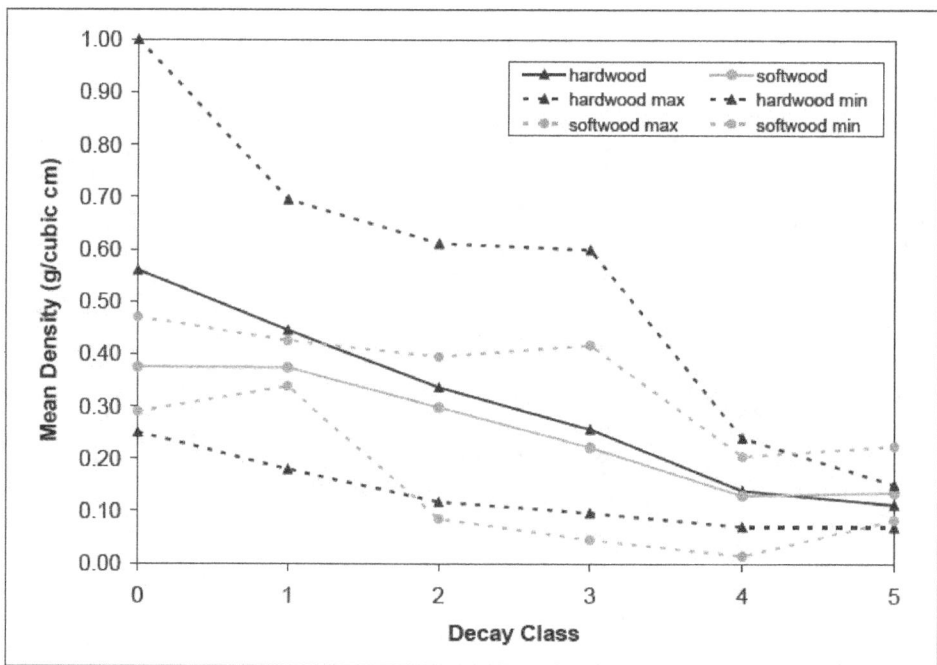

Figure 2.—Density of hardwood versus softwood by decay class. The mean as well as the minimum and maximum for each class are displayed.

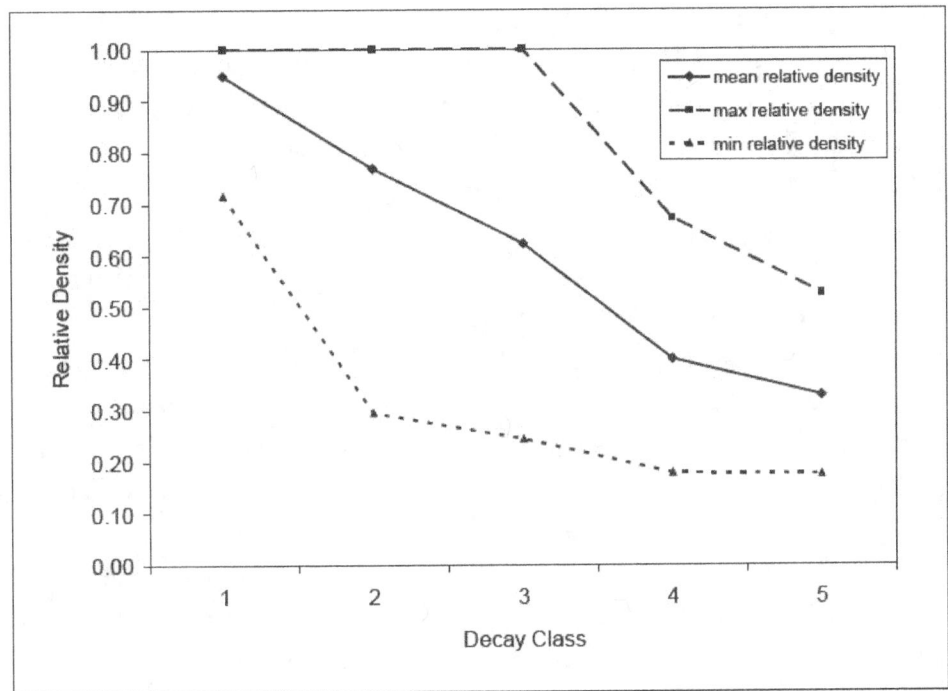

Figure 3.—Relative density of all species by decay class. Each point represents a species that has been sampled for each decay class. The relative density is the observed density divided by the initial or green density.

Although the mean relative density of hardwoods is slightly lower than that of softwoods (Fig. 4), these differences are very small compared to the range in values observed. For example, the relative density of decay class 3 hardwoods is 0.1 relative density units lower than that for softwoods. However, this is approximately one-third the difference between the minimum and the mean for hardwoods. The range for softwoods is lower than that for hardwoods, but as with absolute density it completely overlaps that of hardwoods. This

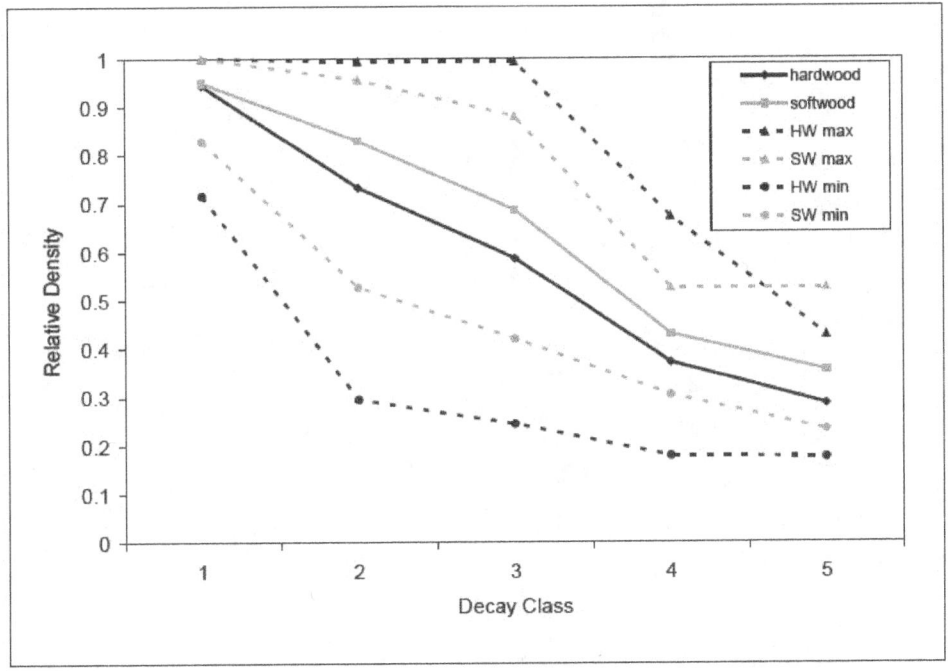

Figure 4.—Relative density of hardwood versus softwood by decay class. The mean as well as the minimum and maximum for each class are displayed.

indicates that separating species by hardwood versus softwood classes will not substantially decrease the uncertainty in prediction of mean relative density. However, separation into these two classes might reduce uncertainty below using the maximum and minimum of all species because the uncertainty range for softwoods is lower than that for hardwoods.

At least 18 temperate genera have been sampled, about half of which contain multiple species. Several patterns of relative density decline are evident in the mean for each genus, which suggests that perhaps stratifying by genus would reduce uncertainty (Fig. 5). However, plotting the minimum and maximum relative density for well-sampled genera indicates there is considerable variation (as much as 0.2 relative density units) within each genus (Fig. 6). This variation is quite high relative to the typical standard error of the mean for a species, which generally ranges from 0.02 to 0.05 relative density units. This indicates that while genus may be used to predict unsampled species, the uncertainty would be as much as tenfold higher than for species that have been sampled.

Examination of the mean of each species indicates a number of repeated patterns in relative density declines (Fig. 7). The simplest pattern, a steady decline in density (hereafter referred to as the S pattern), was observed for 15 species (Fig. 7a). In this case, density appeared to decline by approximately an equal amount between decay classes 1 to 4 and then to a lesser degree from decay class 4 to 5. The most common pattern, a lag followed by steady decline (the

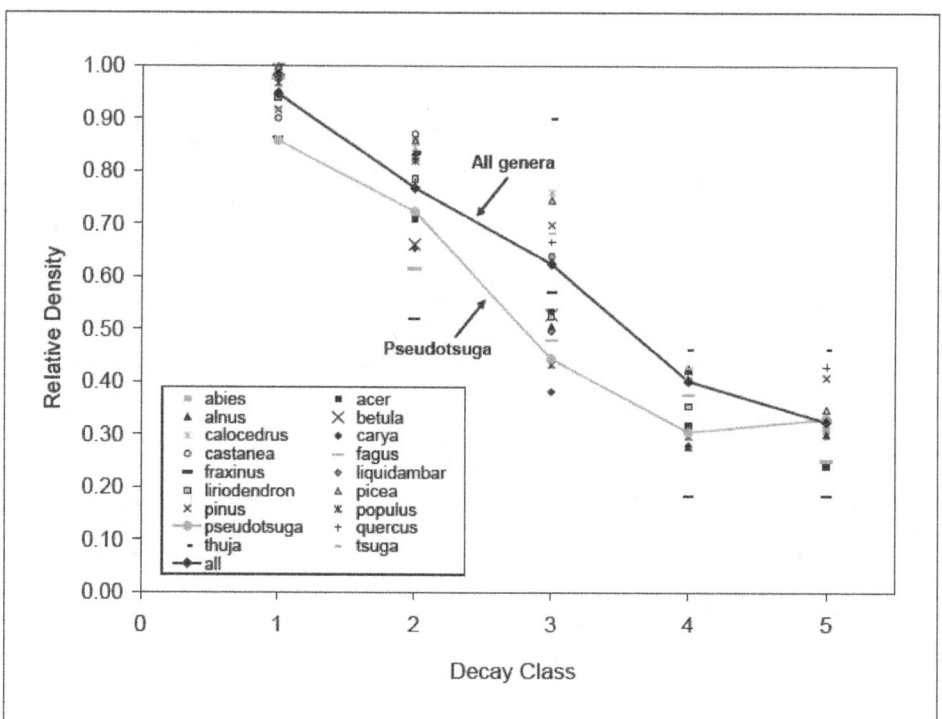

Figure 5.—Mean relative density for common temperate genera.

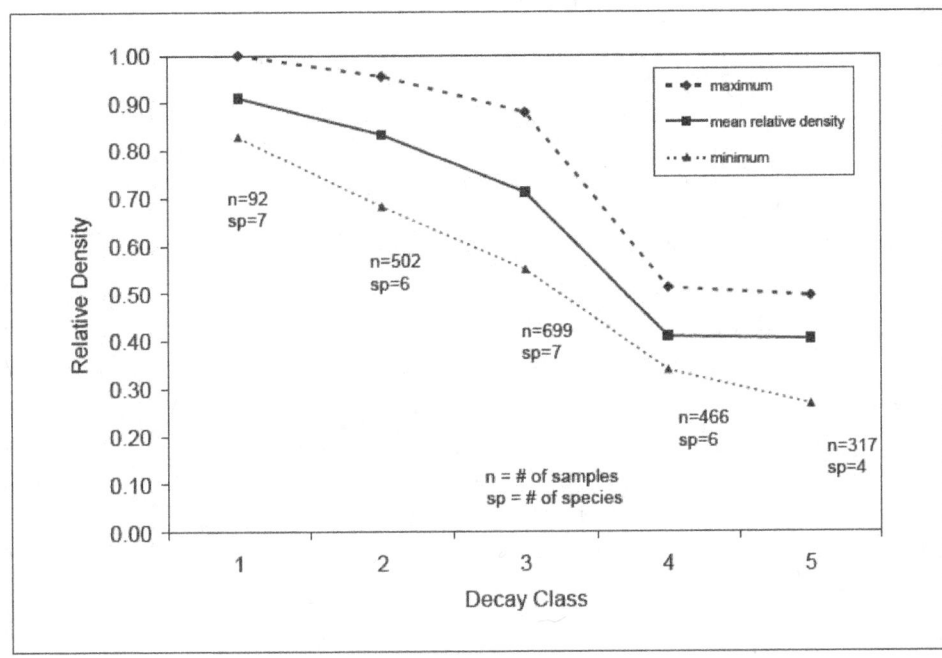

Figure 6.—Examples of the mean, minimum, and maximum relative density for genera that have been well sampled. The number of species and total number of samples for each decay class are noted.

LS pattern), occurred in 30 species (Fig. 7b). In this pattern, decay class 1 is similar in density to fresh wood and then there is a steady decline in density. A lag that lasted into decay class 2 was evident in five species, and this was typically followed by a steady decline of density in decay classes 3 to 5 (the SLS pattern; Fig. 7c). For six species, it appears that a steady decline is followed by an asymptote in decay classes 4 and 5 (the A pattern; Fig. 7d). This pattern is the one followed by Douglas-fir, the most common species used to represent density reduction patterns. The most complex pattern involved an initial decline in density to decay class 1, followed by a mid-plateau, and finally a steady decline in density (the MP pattern; Fig. 7e). This pattern was followed by seven species.

Understanding the causes of these patterns might be helpful in predicting unsampled species. Unfortunately, we can only hypothesize about possible controls of these patterns. It is possible that the lags we observed in the LS and SLS patterns are associated with the progression of exterior indicators of decay versus the loss of wood via decomposition. In species or environments in which the exterior indicators develop quickly relative to the rate of wood decomposition, the interior wood does not have "enough time" to lose density. Thus, a "lag" in density decline appears. Conversely, if exterior indicators take longer to develop, then the wood can decompose to a greater degree and a steady density decline appears. This difference might not be caused by the species per se, but the environment. In cold and wet environments, bole decomposition rates can be very slow due to waterlogging (Harmon et al. 1986). The same limitation would not be evident for leaves, twigs, and branches; therefore, their

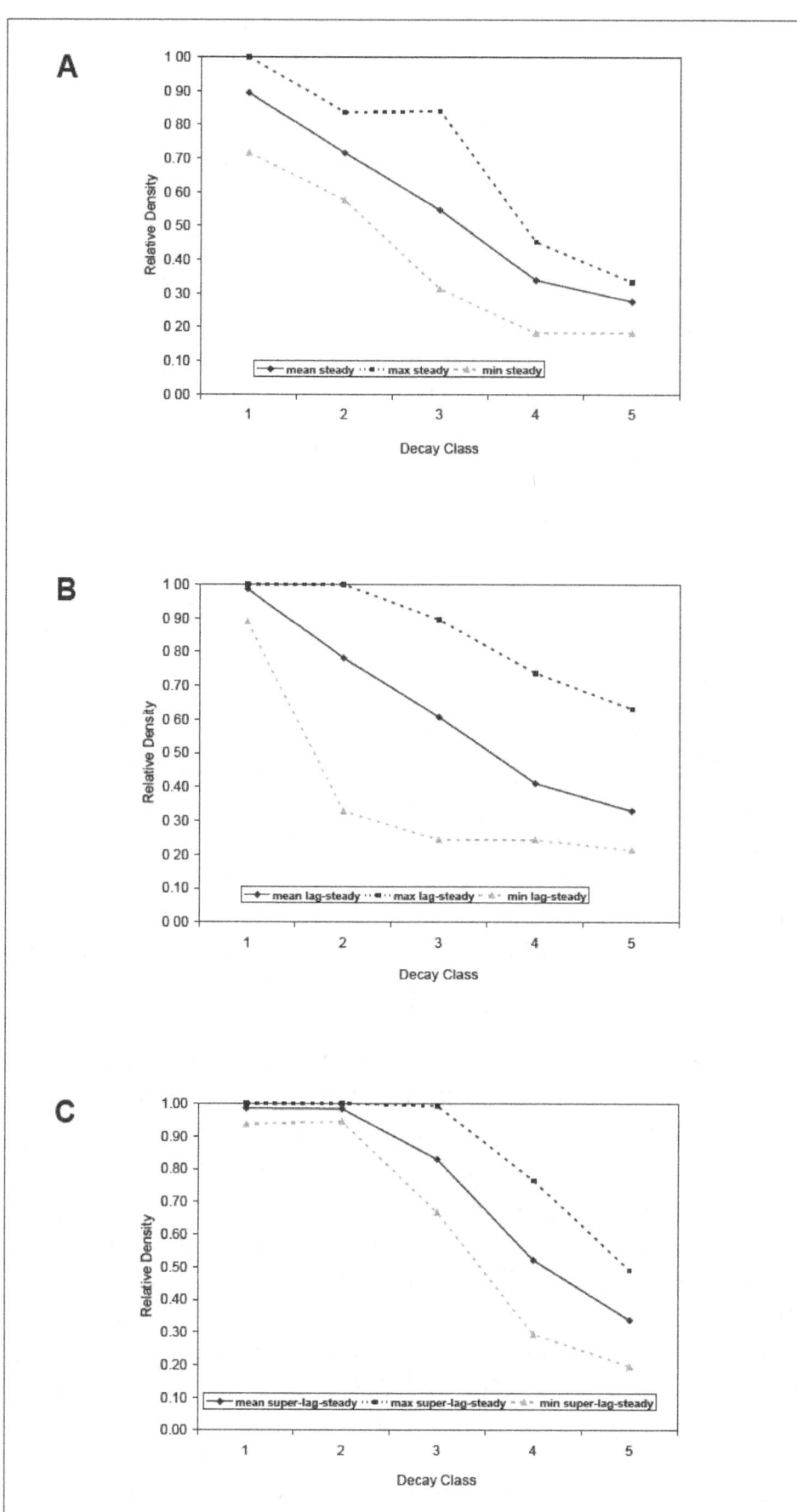

Figure 7.—Relative density reduction patterns. The mean, minimum, and maximum relative densities are presented for each pattern.
A: steady decline (S);
B: lag followed by steady decline (LS);
C: super lag followed by steady decline (SLS).

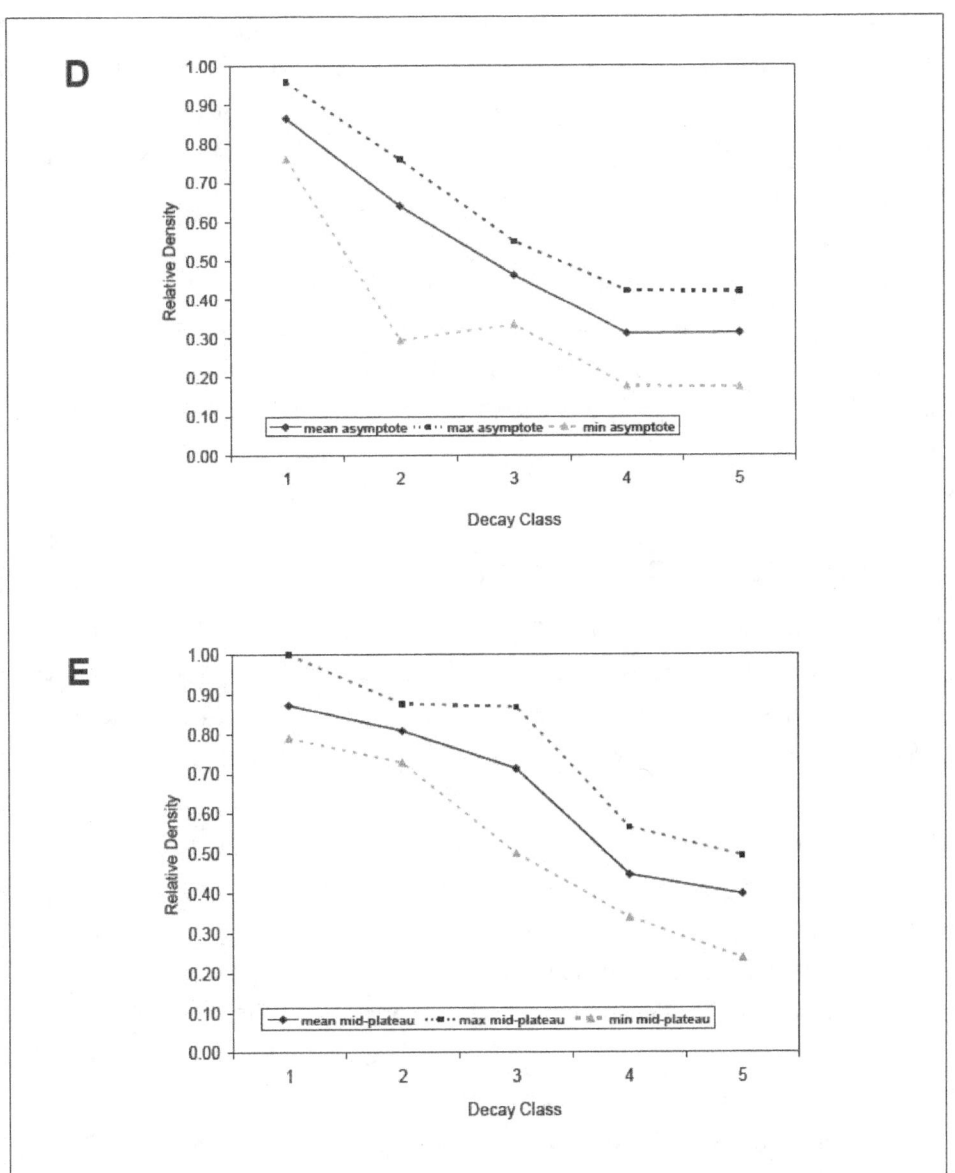

Figure 7 *(continued).*— Relative density reduction patterns. The mean, minimum, and maximum relative densities are presented for each pattern. D: asymptotic (A); E: mid-plateau in density (MP).

decomposition would proceed ahead of the bole's decomposition. The cause of the asymptotic pattern (A) might be related to the presence of a relatively small resistant core of wood, although this is unlikely in the case of Douglas-fir. The most complex pattern, the MP, is possibly associated with a proportionally large amount of highly resistant wood. This would be typified by western redcedar. In this case, sapwood decomposition is quite rapid leading to a decline to decay class 1. The remaining heartwood is, however, very resistant to decay and although certain indicators of decay class 3 develop (e.g., the sloughing of sapwood) the underlying wood remains relatively sound. Eventually this wood begins to decompose and weaken leading to the characteristics typical of decay class 4.

Although these density reduction patterns are useful for descriptive purposes, at this time they cannot be used for predictive purposes. First, as discussed above, the mechanisms causing the differences are not known. Second, determining the degree to which these patterns are statistically different is problematical. In some cases, patterns might differ for only one decay class (e.g., S versus the LS patterns) and therefore for most decay classes they are statistically the same. In others cases, the mean relative density of two patterns are quite different, yet the range for both patterns overlap considerably. Third, while it is logical to hypothesize density reduction patterns would be similar within a genus, we saw little evidence to support that hypothesis in the genera that had been well sampled.

FINE WOODY DEBRIS DENSITY

Relatively few species have had FWD density determined. Our literature search indicated approximately 25 species have been sampled, although some of these "species" represent mixtures named after a dominant species. Most studies appear to have been from northern regions.

The density of undecayed or green FWD decreased as diameter increased (Fig. 8). For example, in the smallest size class (0-8 mm diameter) the mean density of undecayed FWD was 0.61 g/cm^3. In contrast, for the largest size class (25 to 76 mm diameter) the mean undecayed density was 0.50 g/cm^3. Regardless of diameter, undecayed density was highly variable with values ranging between 0.1 and 0.95 g/cm^3. Given the few species in which undecayed FWD has been determined, the ratio of undecayed branch density to bole wood density is a useful variable from which to predict the undecayed FWD density of species that have not yet been studied. These ratios also decline as diameter size class increases, reflecting the decrease in FWD density as the size class increases (Fig. 9).

Density of decayed FWD also decreases as diameter size class increases (Fig. 10) from 0.44 to 0.38 g/cm^3 from the smallest to largest size classes. Relative density of FWD as indicated by ratios of decayed to undecayed pieces increases as size class increases (Fig. 11). This indicates that large diameter pieces are less decomposed than smaller ones. Specifically, the largest pieces have a mean relative density of 0.88, whereas the smallest ones have a mean relative density of 0.61. This might be caused by the increased surface area to volume ratio of the smaller pieces, which might allow faster colonization by agents of decomposition.

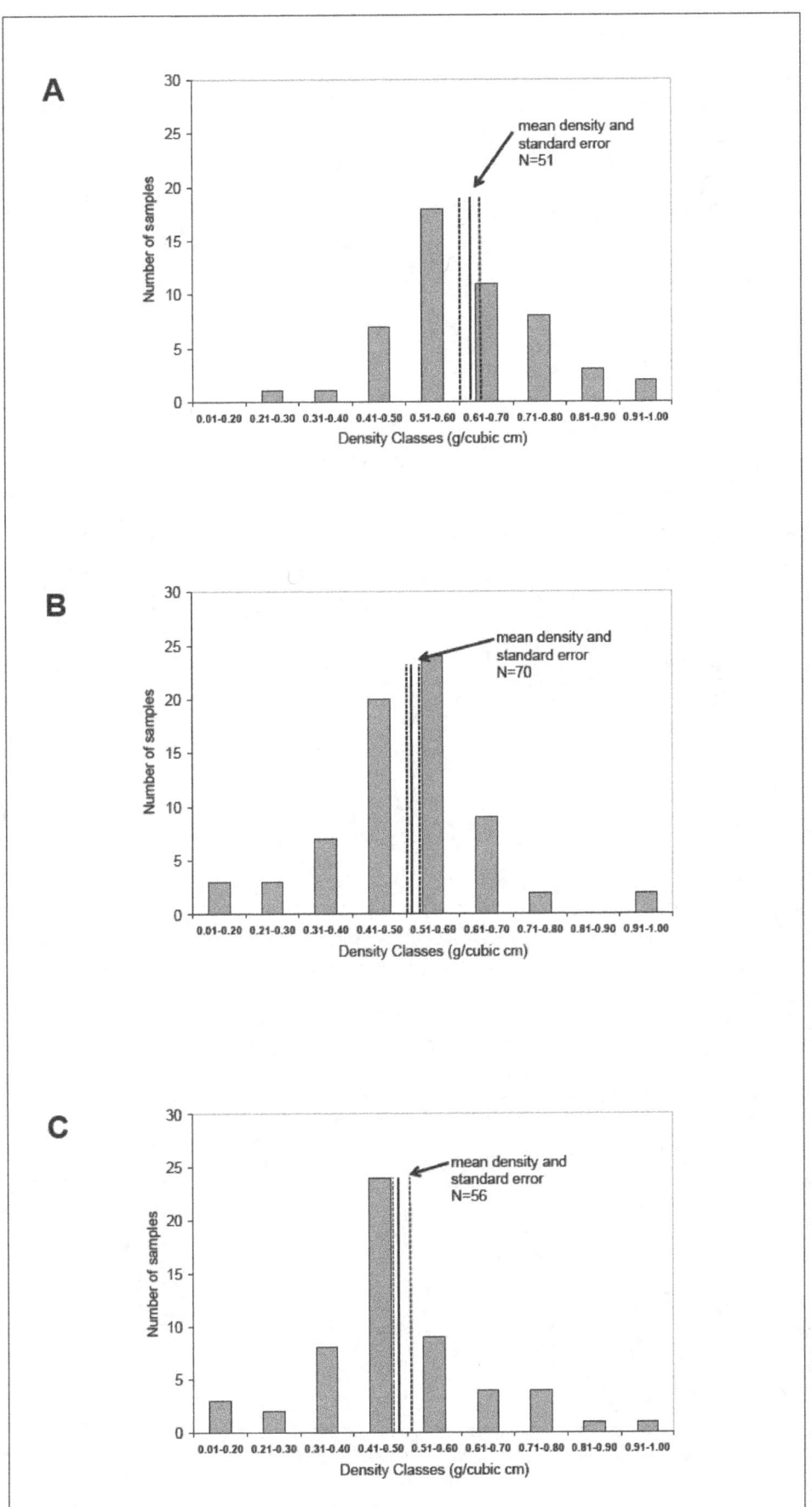

Figure 8.—Distribution of density of undecayed pieces of FWD for three size classes.
(A) 0-1 cm, (B) 1-5 cm, (C) 5-12 cm.

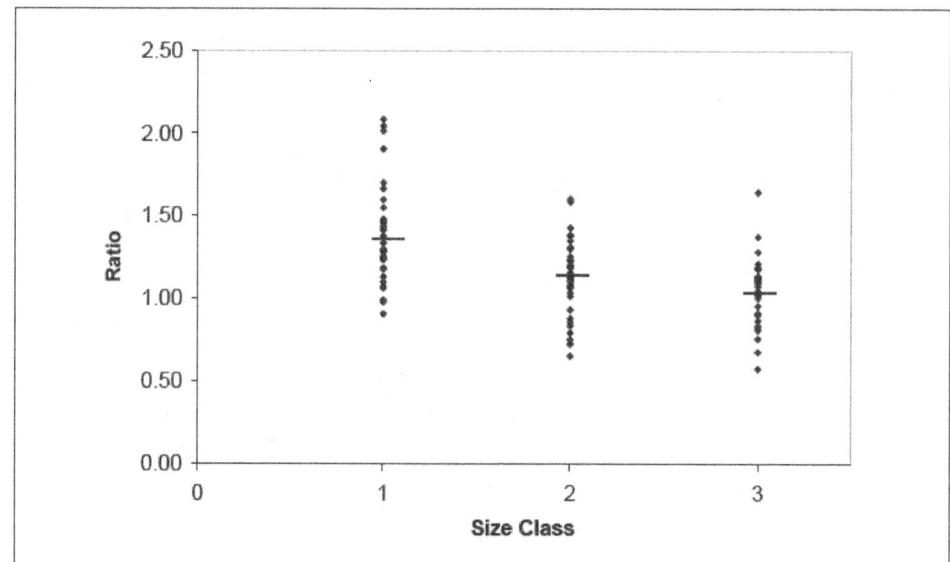

Figure 9.—Observed ratios of green or undecayed bole to branch density for three size classes (1=0-1 cm, 2=1-5 cm, 3=5-12 cm).

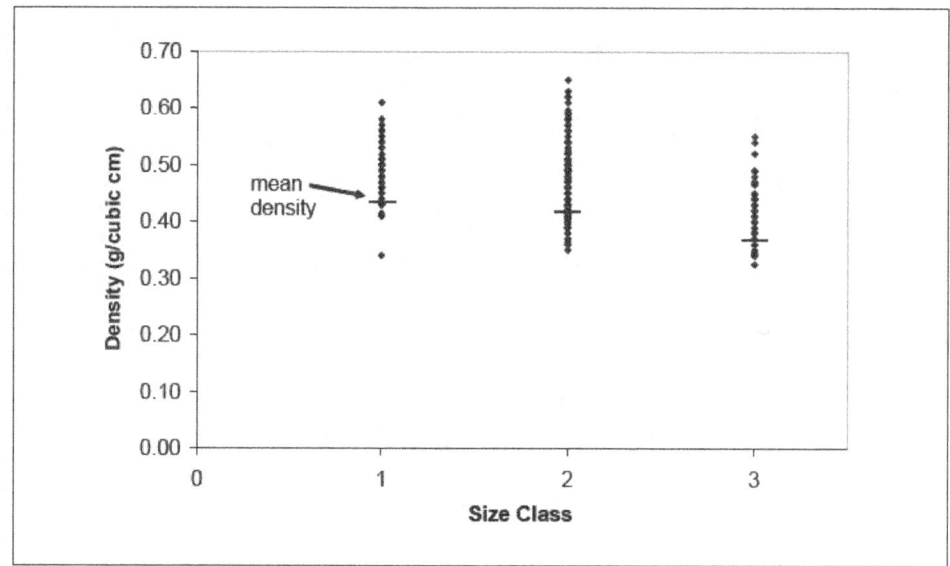

Figure 10.—Density of decayed FWD pieces for three size classes (1=0-1 cm, 2=1-5 cm, 3=5-12 cm).

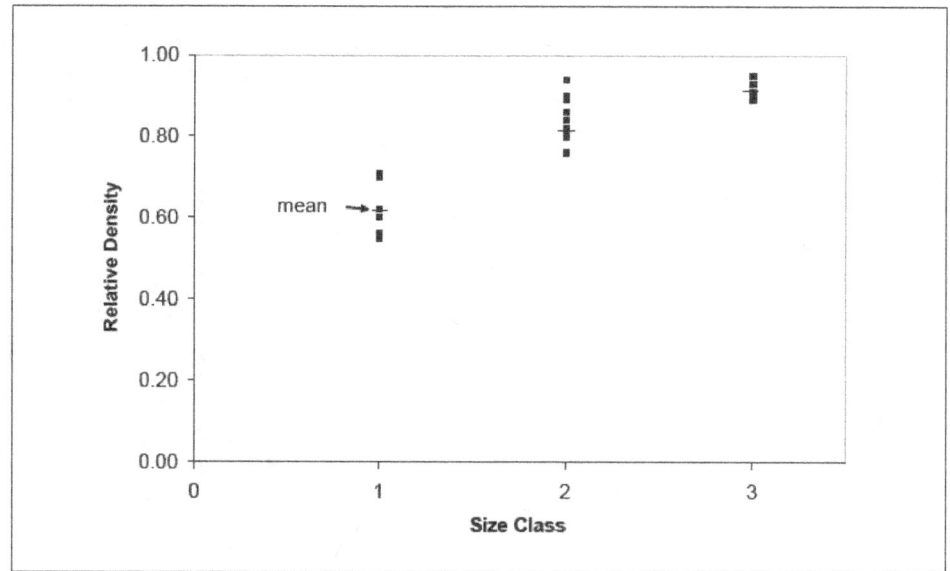

Figure 11.—Relative density of decayed FWD for three size classes (1=0-1 cm, 2=1-5 cm, 3=5-12 cm).

UNCERTAINTIES OF CWD MASS ESTIMATES

Douglas-fir has been the most commonly used species to estimate decay class densities of unsampled species based on the assumption that all species density reduction patterns are similar. Using this as a standard to assess the differences with other possible density reduction patterns indicates that considerable error might have been introduced into CWD biomass estimates (Fig. 12). The size of the error depends on both the density reduction pattern and the volume distribution. For example, if the steady density decline pattern (S) actually occurred, then depending on the distribution of volume for the decay classes, the CWD mass might have been 4 to 12 percent higher than calculated using the Douglas-fir density reduction pattern. While many of these volume distributions are theoretical, it is important to note that the observed volume distribution indicated using Douglas-fir density reduction patterns would have led to 12 percent less CWD biomass than was actually there if the S density reduction pattern was followed. Likewise for the LS pattern (lag-steady), there might have been 20 to 35 percent more CWD biomass present than calculated using Douglas-fir density reduction patterns. Douglas-fir density reduction patterns seem to underestimate for the MP (mid-plateau) pattern as well; there might have been 14 to 44 percent more CWD biomass if the MP pattern was followed. As with the S pattern, the largest errors for the LS and MP patterns occurred for the observed distribution. The overall conclusion is that use of Douglas-fir density reduction patterns has probably underestimated CWD biomass in FIA inventories.

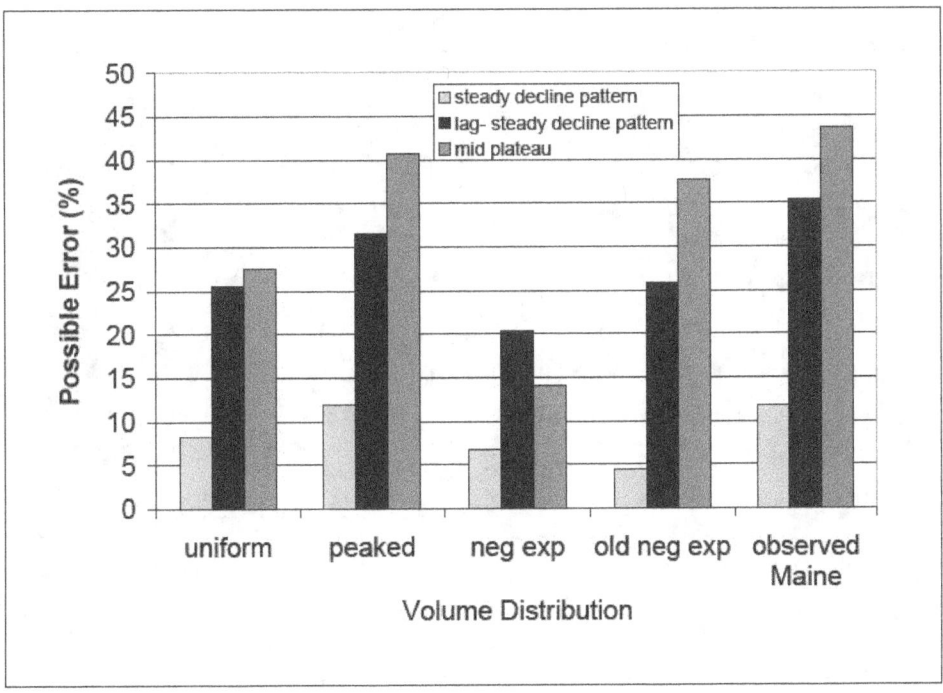

Figure 12.—Uncertainty in CWD mass estimates using various relative density reduction patterns. The differences in two common density reduction patterns relative to that of Douglas-fir in estimated biomass assuming various volume distributions (uniform, peaked, negative exponential, and observed).

Comparison of the uncertainty for a well-sampled species (Douglas-fir) to that when a genus has not been sampled indicates that uncertainty of CWD biomass estimates could be reduced fourfold to tenfold by actually sampling species (Fig. 13). By sampling representative species within a genus, the uncertainty could be reduced by up to 50 percent over not having sampled a genus. Sampling species within a genus could result in a fivefold to sevenfold reduction in uncertainty if values for well-sampled genera (e.g., pines) are typical. Depending on the volume distribution used, uncertainty in CWD biomass for a well-sampled species ranged from ±4 to 7 percent. For a well-sampled genus, the uncertainty ranged from ±21 to 38 percent. In contrast, if a species followed the maximum density reduction pattern, then the estimate of CWD biomass would be 38 to 56 percent higher than if it followed the mean for all species. Similarly, if a species followed the minimum density reduction pattern observed, then the CWD biomass estimated would be 39 to 54 percent lower than if it followed the mean for all species. This indicates that if the density reduction pattern was not known for a genus or species, then there is considerable uncertainty in estimates of CWD mass. Although these uncertainties are a function of the volume distribution assumed, it is important to note that some of the highest uncertainties (±55 percent) were for the observed volume distribution.

UNCERTAINTIES OF FWD MASS ESTIMATES

Our analysis indicated that when FWD relative density is actually measured, the uncertainty is 0.01 to 0.03. Expressed as a percent, this would mean an uncertainty of mass of 1 to 3 percent when species are sampled. In contrast, when

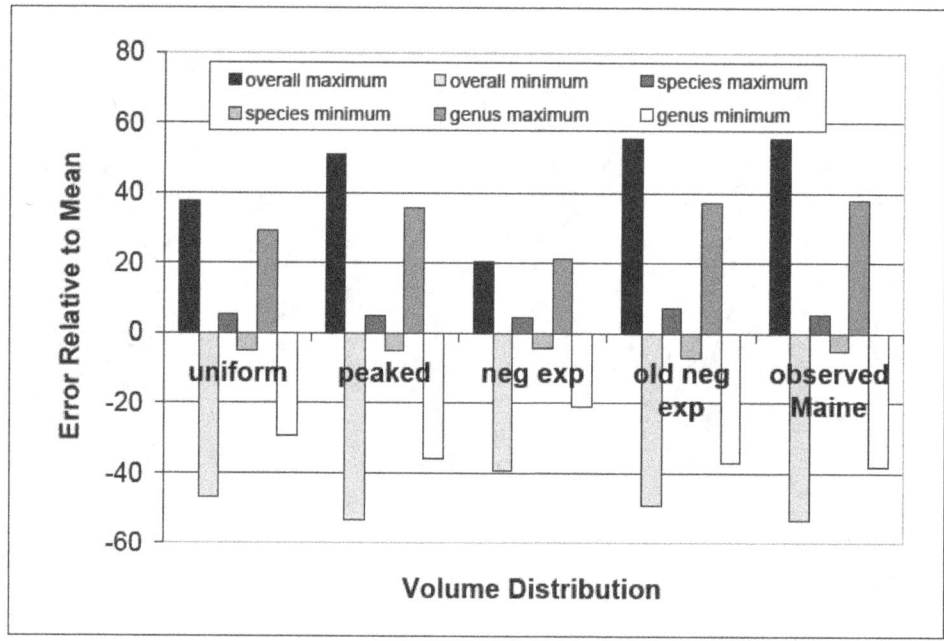

Figure 13.—Uncertainty in CWD mass estimates based on the ranges expected for a well-studied species, a well-studied genus, and all the species sampled. The volume distributions included uniform, peaked, negative exponential, and observed.

relative density has to be estimated, the uncertainty of FWD mass estimation ranges from 12 to 19 percent. Sampling FWD density for species, therefore, would decrease uncertainty by up to an order of magnitude.

These conclusions need to be tempered with the realization that density is likely to vary considerably when pulses of FWD occur. Regardless of the size of the FWD pulse, there was a dip in the FWD relative density (Fig. 14). This was caused by the changing proportion between the pulse-related FWD and that added by regular mortality. Varying the decomposition rate of the pulse of FWD did not influence the range of relative densities that occurred. The larger the size of the pulse, the greater the dip in density as time since the pulse increased. Moreover, as difference between the average and the asymptotic density of the pulse increased, the uncertainty in the FWD relative density also increased. This sensitivity analysis indicates that even if the mean FWD density is known, there are times after disturbances when density could be at least 20 percent higher or lower than the average. For a less conservative set of parameter values, there are times after a disturbance that relative density could be less than half the average relative density. This indicates that the uncertainty introduced by not knowing the history of the stand could introduce as much error as not sampling a species.

BIOMASS TO CARBON CONVERSION FACTORS

There appears to be no consistent trend in carbon concentration as wood decomposes (Tables 1 and 2). The mean carbon concentration of CWD across all decay classes was 49.8 percent; the lowest mean concentration for a decay

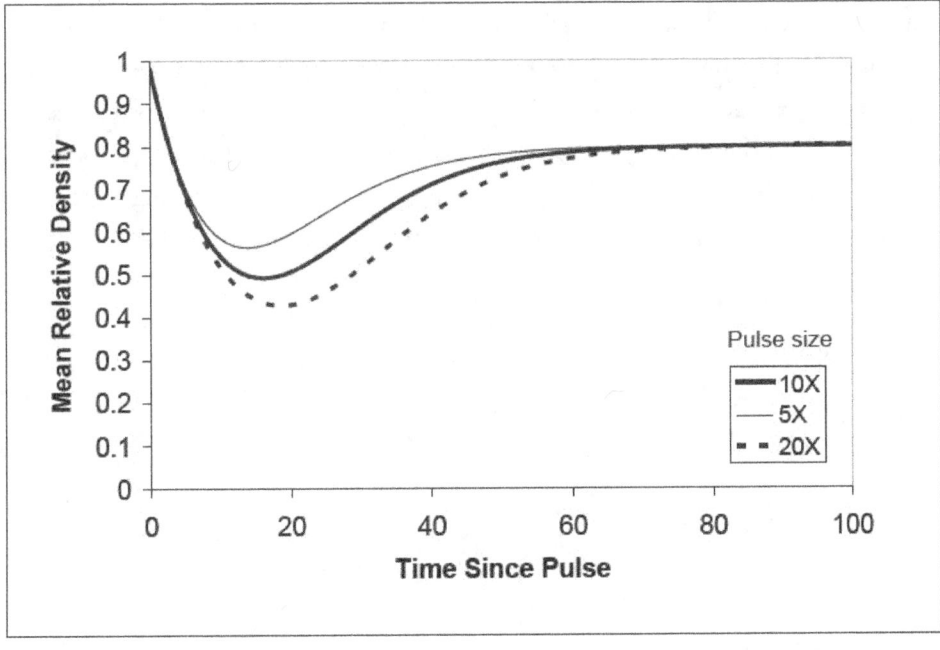

Figure 14.—Possible changes in FWD relative density caused by pulses of undecayed FWD of various sizes relative to background levels. In this case the pulse of FWD was assumed to disappear at a rate of 10 percent a year to a relative density of 0.2. The averaged relative density for FWD from regular mortality processes was assumed to be 0.8. The size of the pulse relative to regular mortality varies between lines.

Table 1.—Biomass to carbon conversion factors for CWD based on percent carbon of samples

Decay class	Mean	Standard error	Minimum	Maximum
		percent carbon		
1	49.9	0.7	47.8	51.5
2	48.8	0.7	42.4	53.6
3	48.6	1.5	42.4	51.6
4	51.8	0.9	48.2	55.2
5	50.1	1.3	41.8	55.2

Source of data: Busse (1994); Currie and Nadelhoffer (2002), Lang and Forman (1978), Harmon et al. (1987), Lambert et al. (1980).

Table 2.—Biomass to carbon conversion factors for FWD based on percent carbon of samples

Decay class	Size class	Mean	Standard error	Minimum	Maximum
	cm		percent carbon		
Undecayed	1.0-2.5	50.8	2.0	51.5	50.3
Undecayed	2.5-5.0	49.8	1.2	50.0	49.5
Undecayed	5.0-10.0	49.1	0.1	49.1	49.1
Decayed	1.0-2.5	51.3	1.9	52.0	50.6
Decayed	2.5-5.0	51.6	2.9	52.4	51.0
Decayed	5.0-10.0	50.5	2.9	50.9	49.8

Source of data: Currie and Nadelhoffer (2002).

class was 48.6 percent and the highest was 51.8 percent. For FWD the mean carbon concentration was 50.8 percent, with a range of 49.1 to 51.6 percent. Although the range of values within decay and size classes was up to 10 percent of the mean, the uncertainty in carbon concentrations used to convert biomass to carbon is very low relative to densities. As a first approximation, using a mean concentration of 50 percent with an uncertainty of 2 percent would be adequate.

DATABASES OF DENSITY ESTIMATES

We have created three databases, two CWD and one FWD, that can be combined with woody detritus volume data to calculate the mass of this material (Appendices 2-4). For both FWD and CWD, we present the density in either absolute or relative terms. In the case of FWD, we report the estimates for absolute and relative density for each of three size classes in one database. For CWD, we report the estimates for the five decay classes in separate absolute and relative density databases. For each estimate, except undecayed CWD, we present a code for the method of estimation, which, as described in the methods, determines the uncertainty of the estimate. While the absolute density values are probably the easiest to use, the relative density values help one understand how the absolute densities were calculated. In addition to an estimate of the most likely value (i.e., the mean or median value depending on how the estimate was made), we also present an uncertainty value. This is analogous to one standard error of the mean; therefore, to approximate the 95 percent confidence intervals, the estimated uncertainty needs to be multiplied by 2 and then added and subtracted from the most likely value.

For both FWD and CWD, most species have not been sampled and therefore the uncertainty is generally high. For CWD, of the 260 species considered by the FIA inventory, 53 (20 percent) have been sampled for at least some decay classes. While sampling more species and genera would improve estimates, it should be noted that many major genera have been sampled. For FWD, very few species-size class combinations have been sampled, with only 25 of the possible 1,046 combinations with actual data. The low proportion of combinations sampled (2 percent) has led to a very high uncertainty in FWD density estimates.

EXAMPLES OF USE

Estimating the most likely value of mass of FWD or CWD is straightforward. If using the relative density values, then one needs to multiply the undecayed density by the relative density for each decay or size class, and then multiply that number by the volume in each decay or size class. Summing the masses for each decay or size class gives the total mass. If using the absolute density database, one multiplies the decay or size class density by the volume in each class and then sums to get the total mass.

Estimating the uncertainty in mass is complex with only an approximation of uncertainty. However, it is better to have some sense of this uncertainty than to not report it. Given that uncertainty can only be approximated, one needs to adopt several guiding principles. The first is that it is better to overestimate than to underestimate uncertainty. Therefore, when there is a choice between using calculation methods that can give either higher versus lower estimates, the higher one should be selected as long as it represents a reasonable set of assumptions. Second, uncertainty estimation in a complex set of calculations can be broken down hierarchically: there is no reason to calculate all uncertainty terms at once. Third, understanding the correlation between variables is important to estimating overall uncertainty because as uncertainty terms for the parts are combined the degree of correlation determines whether the uncertainty is increased or reduced. For example, if all the uncertainties for each decay class are perfectly and positively correlated, then the total uncertainly will be maximized (i.e., the masses are either all the minimums or all the maximum masses). If, on the other hand, the uncertainties are perfectly and negatively correlated, then the total uncertainty will be minimized (i.e., some maximum masses are being offset by minimum masses). When there is no correlation between uncertainties in the decay classes, then the total uncertainty is intermediate. In the case of woody detritus mass estimates, the least likely case would be for all the uncertainties to be negatively correlated because there is no specific mechanism to cause this pattern.

Given the complexity of the problem there is no single formula to estimate uncertainty. One method would be to perform a Monte Carlo analysis drawing from the distributions for the decay- and size-class databases. As an alternative, we combine uncertainties using calculations based on summary statistics. In the following sections, we present a series of calculations to provide examples, but because each project is likely to have data structured in different ways, it is best to use the examples only as guidance and not as a substitute for a project-specific analysis. To provide a hierarchical framework, we start at the finest level of detail (e.g., sampled species) and work toward more assumptions (e.g., unsampled genera). In this particular set of examples, we use subscripts to indicate the level within the hierarchy being considered (DC=decay class; Sp=species; S=site). Our example considers CWD, but a similar set of calculations could be performed for FWD if size classes were also considered. Specific examples for each level in the hierarchy are given in Appendices 5 and 6.

WITHIN A DECAY OR SIZE CLASS FOR A SPECIES AND SITE

To calculate the uncertainty for a decay class for a species at a particular site (or plot), the uncertainty can be estimated by multiplying the volume by the absolute density uncertainty values:

$$\text{Uncertainty Mass}_{DC\text{-}Sp\text{-}S} = \text{Volume}_{DC\text{-}Sp\text{-}S} * \text{Uncertainty Density}_{DC\text{-}Sp\text{-}S}$$

WITHIN A SPECIES AND SITE

To calculate the uncertainty for species with estimated densities at a particular site (or plot), this term can be approximated by adding uncertainty in mass for all the decay classes:

$$\text{Uncertainty Mass}_{Sp\text{-}S} = \Sigma\ \text{Uncertainty Mass}_{DC\text{-}Sp\text{-}S}$$

This assumes there is a perfect positive correlation of uncertainties for the decay classes, which reflects the fact that an unsampled species is systematically underestimated or overestimated in terms of decay class specific densities. In other words, there is a consistent pattern for a species relative to the mean estimates. However, for species that have been sampled, it is likely that there are few systematic differences, and a random relationship would be more appropriate:

$$\text{Uncertainty Mass}_{Sp\text{-}S} = \text{sqrt}\ \Sigma\ (\text{Uncertainty Mass}_{DC\text{-}Sp\text{-}S}{}^2)$$

where the uncertainty of each decay class is squared and then summed. By taking the square root of this term, the total uncertainty for a species within a site can be estimated. This is based on the notion that the square of uncertainties are additive, but the uncertainties are not (i.e., variances are additive).

WITHIN A SPECIES FOR ALL SITES

To calculate the uncertainty for species that have not had density estimated when multiple sites (or plots) are combined, we assume the total uncertainty in mass can be estimated by adding uncertainty in mass for all the sites or plots:

$$\text{Uncertainty Mass}_{Sp} = \Sigma \text{ Uncertainty Mass}_{Sp-S}$$

This assumes a perfect positive correlation in uncertainty, which is the most likely case for species that have not been sampled. In this case, all decay classes for a species at all places were likely either underestimated or overestimated to the same degree. For species that have been sampled for density, it is more realistic to assume that the uncertainties are not correlated and the uncertainty represents random variation in the population:

$$\text{Uncertainty Mass}_{Sp} = \text{sqrt } \Sigma \text{ (Uncertainty Mass}_{Sp-S}^{2})$$

where the uncertainty of a species mass for each plot is squared and then summed. By taking the square root of this term, the total uncertainty for the species for all sites can be estimated.

WITHIN A SITE

The uncertainty in mass for a site would combine the mass of all the species at a site. Because there is no reason to believe that uncertainty in one species is correlated with another, the overall uncertainty would be approximated by:

$$\text{Uncertainty Mass}_{S} = \text{sqrt } \Sigma \text{ (Uncertainty Mass}_{Sp-S}^{2})$$

where the uncertainty of each species is squared and then summed. By taking the square root of this term, the total uncertainty within a site can be estimated.

ALL SITES

Assuming that the uncertainty in mass for each species for all sites has been estimated, the uncertainty for all sites would be computed by assuming there is no correlation between sites:

$$\text{Uncertainty Mass}_{T} = \text{sqrt } \Sigma \text{ (Uncertainty Mass}_{Sp}^{2})$$

where the uncertainty of each species for all sites is squared and then summed over all species. Taking the square root of this term gives the total uncertainty at all levels.

FUTURE NEEDS

While the databases we created will be helpful for improving FWD and CWD mass estimates, they have several notable problems that limit their usefulness.

In the case of CWD, it is essential to separate the pieces inventoried into the decay classes. To be effective, the decay classes used in inventories need to be better defined so that they are repeatable. Most decay class systems are based on Douglas-fir decay patterns; however, species can differ in substantial ways. While adjustments inevitably are made in the field, these are not always documented, and therefore uncertainty about their meaning is introduced. This uncertainty could be reduced by consistently describing decay classes so that actual differences between species and locations can be documented.

A more systematic sampling of CWD for species and locations is needed. Past sampling of CWD density has been ad hoc or related to studies of decomposition rates, the main focus of ecological studies. Ideally, all the major species would be studied, the decay classes defined in objective and systematic ways, and the wood density as well as carbon content determined. Currently many major species have not been sampled or decay classes within species have been inadequately sampled (< 5 samples). By sampling the most abundant species, uncertainty of mass estimates could be reduced to approximately 5 percent, a considerable improvement over the current uncertainty, which could be as high as 50 percent.

FWD densities have rarely been sampled and although the current database is a logical starting place, it could be significantly improved. Current publications often do not report sample numbers or variation. Mixtures of species are often reported, and while this makes sense when working within a uniform forest type, it is not efficient when mixtures of species change from place to place. A more flexible system might be derived if species values were reported because mixtures could be created continuously from this data structure. The separation of undecayed versus decayed FWD is helpful in estimating density, but separation of FWD into decay classes would reduce uncertainty. It would probably not be reasonable to classify each piece of FWD into a decay class, but a system to characterize decay state quickly would greatly reduce uncertainties in mass estimation of this pool.

Despite the lack of data on carbon concentrations in decaying wood, our review indicated that this variable does not change greatly with size or degree of decay. Compared to the uncertainty related to wood density, carbon concentrations are relatively certain. While additional sampling would be desirable, it would not be a priority relative to wood density.

Finally, it should be noted that most of these improvements are static in nature: they can be applied to a set of inventory-based volumes, but they do not allow one to incorporate decomposition induced density reductions over time. To make dynamic adjustments, it would be extremely valuable to know the decomposition rates of FWD and CWD. Knowledge of these rates would also allow one to directly estimate fluxes from a single inventory rather than a series of inventories. This information would also allow one to better interpret why inventory estimates are changing over time.

ACKNOWLEDGMENTS

This research was supported by the Forest Inventory and Analysis program and the Pacific Northwest Research Station of the U.S. Forest Service, the Bullard Fellowship of Harvard University, the Oregon State University Richardson Endowment, and the Long-term Ecological Studies of the National Science Foundation.

LITERATURE CITED

Brown, J.K. 1974. Handbook for inventorying downed woody material. Gen. Tech. Rep. INT-16. Ogden, UT: U.S. Department of Agriculture, Forest Service, Intermountain Forest and Range Experiment Station. 24 p.

Burgan, R.E. 1988. 1988 revisions to the 1978 National Fire Danger Rating System. Res. Pap. SE-273. Asheville, NC: U.S. Department of Agriculture, Forest Service, Southeastern Forest Experiment Station. 39 p.

Franklin, J.F.; Shugart, H.H.; Harmon, M.E. 1987. Tree death as an ecological process. Bioscience. 37: 550-556.

Harmon, M.E.; Sexton, J. 1996. Guidelines for measurements of woody detritus in forest ecosystems. Pub. 20. Seattle, WA: University of Washington, U.S. LTER Network Office. 73 p.

Harmon, M.E.; Cromack, K., Jr.; Smith, B.G. 1987. Coarse woody debris in mixed-conifer forests, Sequoia National Park, California. Canadian Journal of Forest Research. 17: 1265-1272.

Harmon, M.E.; Krankina, O.; Sexton, J. 2000. Decomposition vectors: a new approach to estimating woody detritus decomposition dynamics. Canadian Journal of Forest Research. 30: 76-84.

Harmon, M.E.; Franklin, J.F.; Swanson, F.J.; Sollins, P.; Gregory, S.V.; Lattin, J.D.; Anderson, N.H.; Cline, S.P.; Aumen, N.G.; Sedel, J.R.; Lienkamper, G.W.; Cromack, K., Jr.; Cummins, K.W. 1986. Ecology of coarse woody debris in temperate ecosystems. Advances in Ecological Research. 15: 133-302.

Olson, J.S. 1963. Energy storage and the balance of producers and decomposers in ecological systems. Ecology. 44: 322-331.

Sollins, P. 1982. Input and decay of coarse woody debris in coniferous stands in western Oregon and Washington. Canadian Journal of Forest Research. 12: 18-28.

Sollins, P.; Cline, S.P.; Verhoeven, T.; Sachs, D.; Spycher, G. 1987. Patterns of log decay in old-growth Douglas-fir forests. Canadian Journal of Forest Research. 17: 1585-1595.

Triska, F.J.; Cromack, K. 1980. The role of wood debris in forests and streams. In: Waring, R.H., ed. Forests: fresh perspectives from ecosystem analysis. Proceedings 40th biology colloquium. Corvallis, OR: Oregon State University Press: 171-190.

U.S. Department of Agriculture. Forest Service. 1999. Wood handbook: wood as an engineering material. Gen. Tech. Rep. FPL-113. Madison, WI: U.S. Department of Agriculture, Forest Service, Forest Products Laboratory. 463 p.

Woodall, C.W.; Lutes, D. 2004. Sensitivity analysis of down woody material data processing routines. In: McRoberts, R.H., ed. Fourth annual FIA science symposium proceedings. Washington, DC: U.S. Department of Agriculture, Forest Service: 199-202.

Woodall, C.W.; Monleon, V.J. 2008. Sampling protocols, estimation, and analysis procedures for down woody materials indicator of the FIA Program. Gen. Tech. Rep. NRS-22. Newtown Square, PA: U.S. Department of Agriculture, Forest Service, Northern Research Station. 68 p.

Yatskov, M.; Harmon, M.E.; Krankina, O.N. 1993. A chronosequence of wood decomposition in the boreal forests of Russia. Canadian Journal of Forest Research. 33: 1211-1226.

APPENDICES

APPENDIX 1.—Literature sources of raw density and carbon concentration data

Adams, M.B.; Owens, D.R. 2001. Specific gravity of coarse woody debris for some central Appalachian hardwood forest species. Res. Pap. NE-716. Newtown Square, PA: U.S. Department of Agriculture, Forest Service, Northeastern Research Station. 4 p.

Brown, J.K. 1974. Handbook for inventorying downed woody material. Gen. Tech. Rep. INT-16. Ogden, UT: U.S. Department of Agriculture, Forest Service, Intermountain Forest and Range Experiment Station. 24 p.

Busse, M.D. 1994. Downed bole-wood decomposition in lodgepole pine forests of central Oregon. Soil Science Society of America Journal. 58: 221-227.

Chojnacky, D.C.; Mickler, R.A.; Heath, L.S.; Woodall, C.W. 2004. Estimates of down woody materials in eastern U.S. forests. Environmental Management. 33: (Supplement 1) S44-S55.

Currie, W.S.; Nadelhoffer, K.J. 2002. The imprint of land-use history: patterns of carbon and nitrogen in downed woody debris at the Harvard Forest. Ecosystems. 5: 446-460.

Duvall, M.D.; Grigal, D.F. 1999. Effects of timber harvesting on coarse woody debris in red pine forests across the Great Lakes states, U.S.A. Canadian Journal of Forest Research. 29: 1926-1934.

Erickson, H.E.; Edmonds, R.L.; Peterson, C.E. 1985. Decomposition of logging residues in Douglas-fir western hemlock, Pacific silver fir, and ponderosa pine systems. Canadian Journal of Forest Research. 15: 914-921.

Fahey, T.J. 1983. Nutrient dynamics of aboveground detritus in lodgepole pine (*pinus contorta* ssp. *latifolia*) ecosystems, southeastern Wyoming. Ecological Monographs. 53(1): 51-72.

Forrester, J.A.; Runkle, J.R. 2000. Mortality and replacement patterns of an old-growth *Acer-Fagus* woods in the Holden Arboretum, northeastern Ohio. American Midland Naturalist. 144(2): 227-242.

Fraver, S.; Wagner, R.G.; Day, M. 2002. Dynamics of coarse woody debris following gap harvesting in the Acadian forest of Central Maine, U.S.A. Canadian Journal of Forest Research. 32: 2094-2105.

Gerald, E.L.; Forman, R.T.T. 1978. Detrital dynamics in a mature oak forest: Hutcheson Memorial Forest, New Jersey. Ecology. 59(3): 580-595.

Graham, R.L.; Cromack, K., Jr. 1982. Mass, nutrient content, and decay state of dead boles in rain forests of Olympic National Park. Canadian Journal of Forest Research. 12: 511-521.

Hale, C.M.; Pastor, J. 1998. Nitrogen content, decay rates, and decompositional dynamics of hollow versus solid hardwood logs in hardwood forests of Minnesota, U.S.A. Canadian Journal of Forest Research. 28: 1276-1285.

Harmon, M.E.; Sexton, J. 1996. Guidelines for measurements of woody detritus in forest ecosystems. Pub. 20. Seattle, WA: University of Washington, U.S. LTER Network Office. 73 p.

Harmon, M.E.; Cromack, K., Jr.; Smith, B.G. 1987. Coarse woody debris in mixed-conifer forests, Sequoia National Park, California. Canadian Journal of Forest Research. 17: 1265-1272.

Harmon, M.E.; Hennessy, T.; Silsbee, D.G. 1980. Woody fuel dimensions within Great Smoky Mountains National Park. Res./Resour. Manage. Rep. 31. Gatlinburg, TN: U.S. Department of the Interior, National Park Service, Uplands Field Research Lab. 28 p.

Harmon, M.E.; Whigham, D.F.; Sexton, J.; Olmsted, I. 1995. Decomposition and stores of woody detritus in the dry tropical forests of the Northeastern Yucatan Peninsula, Mexico. Biotropica. 27: 305-316

Hicks, W.T. 1995. Tree mortality, coarse woody debris and the equilibrium status of an old-growth *fagus-acer* forest in southwestern Ohio. Oxford, OH: Miami University. 47 p. M.S. thesis.

Lambert, R.L.; Lang, G.E.; Reiners, W.A. 1980. Loss of mass and chemical change in decaying boles of a subalpine balsam fir forest. Ecology. 61(6): 1460-1473.

Lang, G.E.; Forman, R.T. 1978. Detrital dynamics in a mature oak forest: Hutcheson Memorial Forest, New Jersey. Ecology. 59(3): 580-595.

MacMillan, P.C. 1981. Log decomposition in Donaldson's woods, Spring Mill State Park, Indiana. American Midland Naturalist. 106(2): 335-344.

Nalder, I.A.; Wein, R.W.; Alexander, M.E.; de Groot, W.J. 1997. Physical properties of dead and downed round-wood fuels in the boreal forests of Alberta and Northwest Territories. Canadian Journal of Forest Research. 27: 1513-1517.

Nalder, I.A.; Wein, R.W.; Alexander, M.E.; de Groot, W.J. 2000. Physical properties of dead and downed round-wood fuels in the boreal forests of western and northern Canada. International Journal of Wildland Fire. 9: 85-99.

Pittman, J.R. 2005. Coarse woody debris in industrially managed *Pinus taeda* plantations of the southeastern United States. Blacksburg, VA: Virginia Polytechnic Institute and State University. M.S. thesis. 114 p.

Roussopoulos, P.J.; Johnson, V.J. 1973. Estimating slash fuel loading for several Lake States tree species. Res. Pap. NC-88. St. Paul, MN: U.S. Department of Agriculture, Forest Service, North Central Forest Experiment Station. 8 p.

Ryan, K.C.; Pickford, S.G. 1978. Physical properties of woody fuels in the Blue Mountains of Oregon and Washington. Res. Note PNW-315. Portland, OR: U.S. Department of Agriculture, Forest Service, Pacific Northwest Forest and Range Experiment Station. 9 p.

Sollins P.; Cline, S.P.; Verhoeven, T.; Sachs, D.; Spycher, G. 1987. Patterns of log decay in old-growth Douglas-fir forest. Canadian Journal of Forest Research. 17: 1585-1595.

Wendy, H.L.; Bryant, D.M.; Hutyra, L.R.; Saleska, S.R.; Hammond-Pyle, E.; Curran, D.; Wofsy, S.C. 2006. Woody debris contribution to the carbon budget of selectively logged and maturing mid-latitude forests. Oecologia. 148: 108-117.

APPENDIX 2.—CWD absolute density and its uncertainty for each decay class by species present in the U.S. FIA system

Genus	Species	code	den0	den1	unc1	cod1	den2	unc2	cod2	den3	unc3	cod3	den4	unc4	cod4	den5	unc5	cod5
Abies	amabilis	ABAM	0.400	0.360	0.047	A	0.332	0.022	A	0.212	0.090	B	0.142	0.058	B	0.106	0.025	B
Abies	balsamea	ABBA	0.340	0.360	0.061	A	0.360	0.020	A	0.290	0.042	A	0.170	0.100	A	0.100	0.030	A
Abies	bracteata	ABBR	0.360	0.371	0.058	B	0.308	0.087	B	0.212	0.090	B	0.142	0.058	B	0.106	0.025	B
Abies	concolor	ABCO	0.370	0.340	0.019	A	0.277	0.018	A	0.121	0.014	A	0.138	0.016	A	0.122	0.020	A
Abies	fraseri	ABFR	0.340	0.371	0.058	B	0.308	0.087	B	0.212	0.090	B	0.142	0.058	B	0.106	0.025	B
Abies	grandis	ABGR	0.350	0.341	0.003	A	0.294	0.021	A	0.225	0.018	A	0.142	0.058	B	0.106	0.025	B
Abies	lasiocarpa	ABLA	0.310	0.371	0.028	A	0.288	0.078	A	0.233	0.023	A	0.152	0.030	A	0.117	0.011	A
Abies	magnifica	ABMA	0.360	0.478	0.013	A	0.378	0.053	A	0.150	0.019	A	0.143	0.014	A	0.084	0.010	A
Abies	magnifica var. shastensis	ABMA2	0.360	0.371	0.058	B	0.308	0.087	B	0.212	0.090	B	0.142	0.058	B	0.106	0.025	B
Abies	procera	ABPR	0.370	0.368	0.008	A	0.269	0.009	A	0.235	0.013	A	0.150	0.027	A	0.106	0.025	B
Abies	species	ABIE	0.340	0.371	0.058	B	0.308	0.087	B	0.212	0.090	B	0.142	0.058	B	0.106	0.025	B
Acacia	species	ACSP2	0.600	0.533	0.233	C	0.422	0.263	C	0.325	0.261	C	0.212	0.175	C	0.158	0.077	C
Acer	barbatum	ACBA	0.540	0.536	0.081	B	0.377	0.078	B	0.281	0.075	B	0.177	0.033	B	0.135	0.077	B
Acer	glabrum	ACGL	0.440	0.536	0.081	B	0.377	0.078	B	0.281	0.075	B	0.177	0.033	B	0.135	0.077	B
Acer	grandidentatum	ACGR	0.440	0.536	0.081	B	0.377	0.078	B	0.281	0.075	B	0.177	0.033	B	0.135	0.077	B
Acer	macrophyllum	ACMA	0.440	0.536	0.081	B	0.377	0.078	B	0.281	0.075	B	0.177	0.033	B	0.135	0.077	B
Acer	negundo	ACNE	0.440	0.536	0.081	B	0.377	0.078	B	0.281	0.075	B	0.177	0.033	B	0.135	0.077	B
Acer	nigrum	ACNI	0.520	0.536	0.081	B	0.377	0.078	B	0.281	0.075	B	0.177	0.033	B	0.135	0.077	B
Acer	pensylvanicum	ACPE	0.440	0.536	0.081	B	0.377	0.078	B	0.281	0.075	B	0.177	0.033	B	0.135	0.077	B
Acer	rubrum	ACRU	0.490	0.436	0.050	A	0.260	0.064	A	0.198	0.075	A	0.177	0.033	A	0.135	0.077	B
Acer	saccharinum	ACSA2	0.440	0.536	0.081	B	0.377	0.078	B	0.281	0.075	B	0.177	0.033	B	0.135	0.077	B
Acer	saccharum	ACSA	0.560	0.679	0.028	A	0.452	0.063	A	0.324	0.043	A	0.182	0.014	A	0.150	0.015	A
Acer	species	ACER	0.490	0.536	0.081	B	0.377	0.078	B	0.281	0.075	B	0.177	0.033	B	0.135	0.077	B
Acer	spicatum	ACSP	0.440	0.536	0.081	B	0.377	0.078	B	0.281	0.075	B	0.177	0.033	B	0.135	0.077	B
Aesculus	californica	AECA	0.380	0.533	0.233	C	0.422	0.263	C	0.325	0.261	C	0.212	0.175	C	0.158	0.077	C
Aesculus	species	AESP	0.330	0.533	0.233	C	0.422	0.263	C	0.325	0.261	C	0.212	0.175	C	0.158	0.077	C
Ailanthus	altissima	AIAL	0.370	0.533	0.233	C	0.422	0.263	C	0.325	0.261	C	0.212	0.175	C	0.158	0.077	C
Aleurites	fordii	ALFO	0.470	0.533	0.233	C	0.422	0.263	C	0.325	0.261	C	0.212	0.175	C	0.158	0.077	C
Alnus	rubra	ALRU	0.370	0.386	0.008	A	0.326	0.047	A	0.197	0.011	A	0.108	0.008	A	0.117	0.049	A
Alnus	species	ALSP	0.370	0.386	0.233	B	0.326	0.263	B	0.197	0.261	B	0.108	0.175	B	0.117	0.077	B
Amelanchier	species	AMSP	0.660	0.533	0.233	C	0.422	0.263	C	0.325	0.261	C	0.212	0.175	C	0.158	0.077	C
Arbutus	menziesii	ARME	0.580	0.533	0.233	C	0.422	0.263	C	0.325	0.261	C	0.212	0.175	C	0.158	0.077	C
Asimina	triloba	ASTR	0.470	0.533	0.233	C	0.422	0.263	C	0.325	0.261	C	0.212	0.175	C	0.158	0.077	C
Betula	alleghaniensis	BEAL	0.550	0.580	0.076	B	0.403	0.263	B	0.190	0.030	A	0.170	0.020	A	0.110	0.010	A
Betula	lenta	BELE	0.600	0.635	0.069	A	0.420	0.099	A	0.283	0.085	A	0.170	0.175	B	0.110	0.077	B
Betula	lutea	BELU	0.600	0.636	0.043	A	0.385	0.058	A	0.234	0.045	A	0.170	0.175	B	0.110	0.077	B
Betula	nigra	BENI	0.560	0.580	0.076	B	0.403	0.263	B	0.265	0.105	B	0.170	0.175	B	0.110	0.077	B
Betula	occidentalis	BEOC	0.530	0.580	0.076	B	0.403	0.263	B	0.265	0.105	B	0.170	0.175	B	0.110	0.077	B
Betula	papyrifera	BEPA	0.480	0.469	0.052	A	0.403	0.263	B	0.352	0.128	A	0.170	0.175	B	0.110	0.077	B
Betula	papyrifera var. commutata	BEPA2	0.480	0.580	0.076	B	0.403	0.263	B	0.265	0.105	B	0.170	0.175	B	0.110	0.077	B
Betula	populifolia	BEPO	0.450	0.580	0.076	B	0.403	0.263	B	0.265	0.105	B	0.170	0.175	B	0.110	0.077	B
Betula	species	BESP	0.480	0.580	0.076	B	0.403	0.263	B	0.265	0.105	B	0.170	0.175	B	0.110	0.077	B

(Appendix 2 continued on next page)

(Appendix 2 continued)

Genus	Species	code	den0	den1	unc1	cod1	den2	unc2	cod2	den3	unc3	cod3	den4	unc4	cod4	den5	unc5	cod5
Bumelia	lanuginosa	BULA	0.470	0.533	0.233	C	0.422	0.263	C	0.325	0.261	C	0.212	0.175	C	0.158	0.077	C
Calocedrus	decurrens	CADE3	0.370	0.425	0.105	A	0.269	0.055	A	0.231	0.043	A	0.156	0.091	A	0.143	0.106	C
Carpinus	caroliniana	CACA	0.580	0.533	0.233	C	0.422	0.263	C	0.325	0.261	C	0.212	0.175	C	0.158	0.077	C
Carya	aquatica	CAAQ	0.610	0.599	0.058	B	0.409	0.072	B	0.238	0.061	B	0.173	0.175	B	0.151	0.077	B
Carya	cordiformis	CACO	0.600	0.610	0.074	A	0.367	0.074	A	0.249	0.050	A	0.173	0.175	B	0.151	0.077	B
Carya	glabra	CAGL	0.660	0.599	0.058	B	0.409	0.072	B	0.238	0.061	B	0.173	0.175	B	0.151	0.077	B
Carya	illinoensis	CAIL	0.600	0.599	0.058	B	0.409	0.072	B	0.238	0.061	B	0.173	0.175	B	0.151	0.077	B
Carya	laciniosa	CALA	0.620	0.599	0.058	B	0.409	0.072	B	0.238	0.061	B	0.173	0.175	B	0.151	0.077	B
Carya	myristicaeformis	CAMY	0.560	0.599	0.058	B	0.409	0.072	B	0.238	0.061	B	0.173	0.175	B	0.151	0.077	B
Carya	ovata	CAOV	0.640	0.551	0.071	A	0.479	0.087	A	0.308	0.065	A	0.173	0.175	B	0.151	0.077	A
Carya	species	CASP	0.620	0.633	0.031	A	0.417	0.021	A	0.195	0.017	A	0.173	0.027	A	0.151	0.059	A
Carya	texana	CATE	0.540	0.599	0.058	B	0.409	0.072	B	0.238	0.061	B	0.173	0.175	B	0.151	0.077	B
Carya	tomentosa	CATO	0.640	0.601	0.059	A	0.372	0.033	A	0.238	0.061	B	0.173	0.175	B	0.151	0.077	C
Castanea	dentata	CADE	0.400	0.360	0.046	A	0.348	0.038	A	0.255	0.056	A	0.212	0.175	C	0.158	0.077	C
Castanea	ozarkensis	CAOZ	0.400	0.360	0.233	B	0.348	0.263	B	0.255	0.261	B	0.212	0.175	C	0.158	0.077	C
Castanea	pumila	CAPU	0.400	0.360	0.233	B	0.348	0.263	B	0.255	0.261	B	0.212	0.175	C	0.158	0.077	C
Castanopsis	species	CAST	0.420	0.533	0.233	C	0.422	0.263	C	0.325	0.261	C	0.212	0.175	C	0.158	0.077	C
Catalpa	species	CATA	0.380	0.533	0.233	C	0.422	0.263	C	0.325	0.261	C	0.212	0.175	C	0.158	0.077	C
Celtis	laevigata	CELA	0.470	0.533	0.233	C	0.422	0.263	C	0.325	0.261	C	0.212	0.175	C	0.158	0.077	C
Celtis	occidentalis	CEOC	0.490	0.533	0.233	C	0.422	0.263	C	0.325	0.261	C	0.212	0.175	C	0.158	0.077	C
Celtis	species	CESP	0.490	0.533	0.233	C	0.422	0.263	C	0.325	0.261	C	0.212	0.175	C	0.158	0.077	C
Cercis	canadensis	CECA	0.580	0.533	0.233	C	0.422	0.263	C	0.325	0.261	C	0.212	0.175	C	0.158	0.077	C
Cercocarpus	intricatus	CEIN	1.000	0.533	0.233	C	0.422	0.263	C	0.325	0.261	C	0.212	0.175	C	0.158	0.077	C
Cercocarpus	ledifolius	CELE	1.000	0.533	0.233	C	0.422	0.263	C	0.325	0.261	C	0.212	0.175	C	0.158	0.077	C
Cercocarpus	montanus	CEMO	1.000	0.533	0.233	C	0.422	0.263	C	0.325	0.261	C	0.212	0.175	C	0.158	0.077	C
Chamaecyparis	lawsoniana	CHLA	0.390	0.381	0.105	C	0.318	0.245	C	0.257	0.122	C	0.162	0.091	C	0.143	0.106	C
Chamaecyparis	nootkatensis	CHNO	0.420	0.381	0.105	C	0.318	0.245	C	0.257	0.122	C	0.162	0.091	C	0.143	0.106	C
Chamaecyparis	thyoides	CHTH	0.310	0.381	0.105	C	0.318	0.245	C	0.257	0.122	C	0.162	0.091	C	0.143	0.106	C
Cladrastis	lutea	CLLU	0.520	0.533	0.233	C	0.422	0.263	C	0.325	0.261	C	0.212	0.175	C	0.158	0.077	C
Cornus	florida	COFL	0.640	0.533	0.233	C	0.422	0.263	C	0.325	0.261	C	0.212	0.175	C	0.158	0.077	C
Cornus	nuttallii	CONU	0.580	0.533	0.233	C	0.422	0.263	C	0.325	0.261	C	0.212	0.175	C	0.158	0.077	C
Cornus	species	COSP	0.640	0.533	0.233	C	0.422	0.263	C	0.325	0.261	C	0.212	0.175	C	0.158	0.077	C
Cotinus	obovaus	COOB	0.470	0.533	0.233	C	0.422	0.263	C	0.325	0.261	C	0.212	0.175	C	0.158	0.077	C
Crataegus	species	CRSP	0.620	0.533	0.233	C	0.422	0.263	C	0.325	0.261	C	0.212	0.175	C	0.158	0.077	C
Cupressus	species	CUSP	0.440	0.381	0.105	C	0.318	0.245	C	0.257	0.122	C	0.162	0.091	C	0.143	0.106	C
Diospyros	virginiana	DIVI	0.640	0.533	0.233	C	0.422	0.263	C	0.325	0.261	C	0.212	0.175	C	0.158	0.077	C
Eucalyptus	species	EUSP	0.670	0.533	0.233	C	0.422	0.263	C	0.325	0.261	C	0.212	0.175	C	0.158	0.077	C
Fagus	grandifolia	FAGR	0.560	0.570	0.056	A	0.300	0.042	A	0.167	0.032	A	0.240	0.028	A	0.160	0.012	A
Fraxinus	americana	FRAM	0.550	0.475	0.070	A	0.286	0.070	A	0.317	0.048	A	0.212	0.175	C	0.100	0.030	A
Fraxinus	latifolia	FRLA	0.500	0.475	0.233	B	0.317	0.263	B	0.298	0.261	B	0.212	0.175	C	0.100	0.077	B
Fraxinus	nigra	FRNI	0.450	0.475	0.233	B	0.317	0.263	B	0.298	0.261	B	0.212	0.175	C	0.100	0.077	B
Fraxinus	pennsylvanica	FRPE	0.530	0.475	0.233	B	0.317	0.263	B	0.298	0.261	B	0.212	0.175	C	0.100	0.077	B
Fraxinus	profunda	FRPR	0.540	0.475	0.233	B	0.317	0.263	B	0.298	0.261	B	0.212	0.175	C	0.100	0.077	B
Fraxinus	quadrangulata	FRQU	0.530	0.475	0.233	B	0.317	0.263	B	0.298	0.261	B	0.212	0.175	C	0.100	0.077	B

Genus	Species	code	den0	den1	unc1	cod1	den2	unc2	cod2	den3	unc3	cod3	den4	unc4	cod4	den5	unc5	cod5
Fraxinus	species	FRSP	0.540	0.475	0.233	B	0.317	0.263	B	0.298	0.261	B	0.212	0.175	C	0.100	0.077	B
Gleditsia	aquatica	GLAQ	0.600	0.533	0.233	C	0.422	0.263	C	0.325	0.261	C	0.212	0.175	C	0.158	0.077	C
Gleditsia	triacanthos	GLTR	0.600	0.533	0.233	C	0.422	0.263	C	0.325	0.261	C	0.212	0.175	C	0.158	0.077	C
Gordonia	lasianthus	GOLA	0.370	0.533	0.233	C	0.422	0.263	C	0.325	0.261	C	0.212	0.175	C	0.158	0.077	C
Gymnocladus	dioicus	GYDI	0.500	0.533	0.233	C	0.422	0.263	C	0.325	0.261	C	0.212	0.175	C	0.158	0.077	C
Halesia	species	HASP	0.320	0.533	0.233	C	0.422	0.263	C	0.325	0.261	C	0.212	0.175	C	0.158	0.077	C
Ilex	opaca	ILOP	0.500	0.533	0.233	C	0.422	0.263	C	0.325	0.261	C	0.212	0.175	C	0.158	0.077	C
Juglans	cinerea	JUCI	0.360	0.533	0.233	C	0.422	0.263	C	0.325	0.261	C	0.212	0.175	C	0.158	0.077	C
Juglans	species	JUSP	0.510	0.533	0.233	C	0.422	0.263	C	0.325	0.261	C	0.212	0.175	C	0.158	0.077	C
Juglans	nigra	JUNI	0.510	0.533	0.233	C	0.422	0.263	C	0.325	0.261	C	0.212	0.175	C	0.158	0.077	C
Juniperus	monosperma	JUMO	0.450	0.381	0.105	C	0.318	0.245	C	0.257	0.122	C	0.162	0.091	C	0.143	0.106	C
Juniperus	occidentalis	JUOC	0.440	0.381	0.105	C	0.318	0.245	C	0.257	0.122	C	0.162	0.091	C	0.143	0.106	C
Juniperus	species	JUSP2	0.440	0.533	0.233	C	0.422	0.263	C	0.325	0.261	C	0.212	0.175	C	0.158	0.077	C
Larix	laricina	LALA	0.490	0.381	0.105	C	0.318	0.245	C	0.257	0.122	C	0.162	0.091	C	0.143	0.106	C
Larix	lyallii	LALY	0.480	0.381	0.105	C	0.318	0.245	C	0.257	0.122	C	0.162	0.091	C	0.143	0.106	C
Larix	occidentalis	LAOC	0.480	0.381	0.105	C	0.318	0.245	C	0.257	0.122	C	0.162	0.091	C	0.143	0.106	C
Larix	species	LASP	0.440	0.381	0.105	C	0.318	0.245	C	0.257	0.122	C	0.162	0.091	C	0.143	0.106	C
Liquidambar	styraciflua	LIST	0.460	0.450	0.008	A	0.331	0.031	A	0.228	0.025	A	0.212	0.175	C	0.158	0.077	C
Liriodendron	tulipifera	LITU	0.400	0.352	0.042	A	0.275	0.041	A	0.203	0.026	A	0.141	0.055	A	0.158	0.077	C
Lithocarpus	densiflorus	LIDE	0.580	0.533	0.233	C	0.422	0.263	C	0.325	0.261	C	0.212	0.175	C	0.158	0.077	C
Maclura	pomifera	MAPO	0.760	0.533	0.233	C	0.422	0.263	C	0.325	0.261	C	0.212	0.175	C	0.158	0.077	C
Magnolia	acuminata	MAAC	0.450	0.425	0.028	A	0.399	0.084	A	0.250	0.059	A	0.212	0.175	C	0.158	0.077	C
Magnolia	species	MASP	0.450	0.425	0.233	B	0.399	0.263	B	0.250	0.261	B	0.212	0.175	C	0.158	0.077	C
Malus	species	MASP2	0.610	0.533	0.233	C	0.422	0.263	C	0.325	0.261	C	0.212	0.175	C	0.158	0.077	C
Melia	azedarach	MEAZ	0.470	0.533	0.233	C	0.422	0.263	C	0.325	0.261	C	0.212	0.175	C	0.158	0.077	C
Morus	alba	MOAL	0.590	0.533	0.233	C	0.422	0.263	C	0.325	0.261	C	0.212	0.175	C	0.158	0.077	C
Morus	rubra	MORU	0.590	0.533	0.233	C	0.422	0.263	C	0.325	0.261	C	0.212	0.175	C	0.158	0.077	C
Morus	species	MOSP	0.590	0.533	0.233	C	0.422	0.263	C	0.325	0.261	C	0.212	0.175	C	0.158	0.077	C
Nyssa	aquatica	NYAQ	0.460	0.533	0.233	C	0.422	0.263	C	0.325	0.261	C	0.212	0.175	C	0.158	0.077	C
Nyssa	ogeche	NYOG	0.460	0.533	0.233	C	0.422	0.263	C	0.325	0.261	C	0.212	0.175	C	0.158	0.077	C
Nyssa	sylvatica	NYSY	0.460	0.533	0.233	C	0.422	0.263	C	0.325	0.261	C	0.212	0.175	C	0.158	0.077	C
Olneya	tesota	OLTE	1.000	0.533	0.233	C	0.422	0.263	C	0.325	0.261	C	0.212	0.175	C	0.158	0.077	C
Ostrya	virginiana	OSVI	0.630	0.533	0.233	C	0.422	0.263	C	0.325	0.261	C	0.212	0.175	C	0.158	0.077	C
Oxydendrum	arboreum	OXAR	0.500	0.524	0.103	A	0.406	0.034	A	0.337	0.057	A	0.212	0.175	C	0.158	0.077	C
Paulownia	tomentosa	PATO	0.380	0.533	0.233	C	0.422	0.263	C	0.325	0.261	C	0.212	0.175	C	0.158	0.077	C
Persea	borbonia	PEBO	0.510	0.533	0.233	C	0.422	0.263	C	0.325	0.261	C	0.212	0.175	C	0.158	0.077	C
Picea	abies	PIAB	0.380	0.393	0.057	B	0.312	0.040	B	0.280	0.112	B	0.155	0.035	B	0.129	0.106	B
Picea	breweriana	PIBR	0.330	0.393	0.057	B	0.312	0.040	B	0.280	0.112	B	0.155	0.035	B	0.129	0.106	B
Picea	engelmannii	PIEN	0.330	0.393	0.057	B	0.258	0.023	A	0.280	0.112	B	0.117	0.026	A	0.129	0.106	B
Picea	glauca	PIGL2	0.370	0.393	0.057	B	0.312	0.040	B	0.280	0.112	B	0.155	0.035	B	0.129	0.106	B
Picea	lutzii	PILU	0.370	0.376	0.034	A	0.347	0.035	A	0.255	0.067	A	0.151	0.027	A	0.103	0.018	A
Picea	mariana	PIMA	0.380	0.393	0.057	B	0.312	0.040	B	0.280	0.112	B	0.155	0.035	B	0.129	0.106	B
Picea	pungens	PIPU	0.380	0.393	0.057	B	0.312	0.040	B	0.280	0.112	B	0.155	0.035	B	0.129	0.106	B
Picea	rubens	PIRU	0.380	0.406	0.057	A	0.312	0.040	B	0.316	0.112	A	0.155	0.035	B	0.129	0.106	B

(Appendix 2 continued on next page)

Genus	Species	code	den0	den1	unc1	cod1	den2	unc2	cod2	den3	unc3	cod3	den4	unc4	cod4	den5	unc5	cod5
Picea	sitchensis	PISI	0.370	0.410	0.008	A	0.341	0.021	A	0.263	0.021	A	0.192	0.029	A	0.137	0.008	A
Picea	species	PICE	0.380	0.393	0.057	B	0.312	0.040	B	0.280	0.112	B	0.155	0.035	B	0.129	0.106	B
Pinus	albicaulis	PIAL	0.370	0.368	0.031	B	0.324	0.038	B	0.273	0.070	B	0.169	0.055	B	0.171	0.096	B
Pinus	aristata	PIAR	0.370	0.368	0.031	B	0.324	0.038	B	0.273	0.070	B	0.169	0.055	B	0.171	0.096	B
Pinus	arizonica	PIAR2	0.370	0.368	0.031	B	0.324	0.038	B	0.273	0.070	B	0.169	0.055	B	0.171	0.096	B
Pinus	attenuata	PIAT	0.370	0.368	0.031	B	0.324	0.038	B	0.273	0.070	B	0.169	0.055	B	0.171	0.096	B
Pinus	balfouriana	PIBA	0.370	0.368	0.031	B	0.324	0.038	B	0.273	0.070	B	0.169	0.055	B	0.171	0.096	B
Pinus	banksiana	PIBA2	0.400	0.368	0.031	B	0.324	0.038	B	0.273	0.070	B	0.169	0.055	B	0.171	0.096	B
Pinus	clausa	PICL	0.460	0.368	0.031	B	0.324	0.038	B	0.273	0.070	B	0.169	0.055	B	0.171	0.096	B
Pinus	contorta	PICO	0.380	0.378	0.020	A	0.367	0.013	A	0.276	0.022	A	0.169	0.019	A	0.164	0.009	A
Pinus	coulteri	PICO2	0.370	0.368	0.031	B	0.324	0.038	B	0.273	0.070	B	0.169	0.055	B	0.171	0.096	B
Pinus	discolor	PIDI	0.500	0.368	0.031	B	0.324	0.038	B	0.273	0.070	B	0.169	0.055	B	0.171	0.096	B
Pinus	echinata	PIEC	0.470	0.368	0.031	B	0.324	0.038	B	0.273	0.070	B	0.169	0.055	B	0.171	0.096	B
Pinus	edulis	PIED	0.500	0.368	0.031	B	0.324	0.038	B	0.273	0.070	B	0.169	0.055	B	0.171	0.096	B
Pinus	elliotti	PIEL	0.540	0.368	0.031	B	0.324	0.038	B	0.273	0.070	B	0.169	0.055	B	0.171	0.096	B
Pinus	engelmannii	PIEN2	0.370	0.368	0.031	B	0.324	0.038	B	0.280	0.071	B	0.169	0.055	B	0.129	0.018	B
Pinus	flexilis	PIFL	0.370	0.368	0.031	B	0.324	0.038	B	0.273	0.070	B	0.169	0.055	B	0.171	0.096	B
Pinus	glabra	PIGL	0.410	0.393	0.046	B	0.312	0.040	B	0.280	0.071	B	0.155	0.035	B	0.129	0.018	B
Pinus	jeffreyi	PIJE	0.370	0.365	0.026	A	0.358	0.042	A	0.217	0.047	A	0.205	0.039	A	0.171	0.096	B
Pinus	lambertiana	PILA	0.340	0.369	0.037	A	0.267	0.011	A	0.155	0.020	A	0.122	0.025	A	0.110	0.134	A
Pinus	leiophylla	PILE	0.370	0.368	0.031	B	0.324	0.038	B	0.273	0.070	B	0.169	0.055	B	0.171	0.096	B
Pinus	monophylla	PIMO	0.500	0.368	0.031	B	0.324	0.038	B	0.273	0.070	B	0.169	0.055	B	0.171	0.096	B
Pinus	monticola	PIMO3	0.350	0.344	0.005	A	0.303	0.012	A	0.308	0.015	A	0.169	0.055	B	0.171	0.096	B
Pinus	muricata	PIMU	0.370	0.368	0.031	B	0.324	0.038	B	0.273	0.070	B	0.169	0.055	B	0.171	0.096	B
Pinus	nigra	PINI	0.410	0.368	0.031	B	0.324	0.038	B	0.273	0.070	B	0.169	0.055	B	0.171	0.096	B
Pinus	palustris	PIPA	0.540	0.368	0.031	B	0.324	0.038	B	0.273	0.070	B	0.169	0.055	B	0.171	0.096	B
Pinus	ponderosa	PIPO	0.380	0.338	0.005	A	0.333	0.018	A	0.330	0.035	A	0.129	0.008	A	0.188	0.134	A
Pinus	pungens	PIPU2	0.490	0.393	0.046	B	0.312	0.040	B	0.280	0.071	B	0.155	0.035	B	0.129	0.018	B
Pinus	radiata	PIRA	0.370	0.368	0.031	B	0.324	0.038	B	0.273	0.070	B	0.169	0.055	B	0.171	0.096	B
Pinus	resinosa	PIRE	0.410	0.340	0.046	A	0.324	0.038	B	0.270	0.070	A	0.150	0.055	A	0.110	0.134	A
Pinus	rigida	PIRI	0.470	0.368	0.031	B	0.324	0.038	B	0.273	0.070	B	0.169	0.055	B	0.171	0.096	B
Pinus	sabiniana	PISA	0.370	0.368	0.031	B	0.324	0.038	B	0.273	0.070	B	0.169	0.055	B	0.171	0.096	B
Pinus	serotina	PISE	0.510	0.368	0.031	B	0.324	0.038	B	0.273	0.070	B	0.169	0.055	B	0.171	0.096	B
Pinus	strobiformis	PIST2	0.350	0.368	0.031	B	0.324	0.038	B	0.273	0.070	B	0.169	0.055	B	0.171	0.096	B
Pinus	strobus	PIST	0.340	0.368	0.031	B	0.324	0.038	B	0.273	0.070	B	0.169	0.055	B	0.171	0.096	B
Pinus	sylvestris	PISY	0.410	0.368	0.031	B	0.324	0.038	B	0.273	0.070	B	0.169	0.055	B	0.171	0.096	B
Pinus	taeda	PITA	0.470	0.386	0.012	A	0.306	0.005	A	0.229	0.002	A	0.193	0.004	A	0.224	0.134	A
Pinus	virginiana	PIVI	0.450	0.368	0.031	B	0.324	0.038	B	0.273	0.070	B	0.169	0.055	B	0.171	0.096	B
Planera	aquatica	PLAQ	0.530	0.533	0.233	C	0.422	0.263	C	0.325	0.261	C	0.212	0.175	C	0.158	0.077	C
Platanus	occidentalis	PLOC	0.460	0.533	0.233	C	0.422	0.263	C	0.325	0.261	C	0.212	0.175	C	0.158	0.077	C
Populus	alba	POAL	0.370	0.353	0.233	B	0.422	0.263	C	0.299	0.261	B	0.160	0.175	B	0.110	0.077	B
Populus	angustifolia	POAN	0.340	0.353	0.233	B	0.422	0.263	C	0.299	0.261	B	0.160	0.175	B	0.110	0.077	B
Populus	balsamifera	POBA	0.310	0.353	0.233	B	0.422	0.263	C	0.299	0.261	B	0.160	0.175	B	0.110	0.077	B
Populus	deltoides	PODE	0.370	0.353	0.233	B	0.422	0.263	C	0.299	0.261	B	0.160	0.175	B	0.110	0.077	B

Genus	Species	code	den0	den1	cod1	unc1	den2	unc2	cod2	den3	unc3	cod3	den4	unc4	cod4	den5	unc5	cod5
Populus	fremontii	POFR	0.340	0.353	B	0.233	0.422	0.263	C	0.299	0.261	B	0.160	0.175	B	0.110	0.077	B
Populus	grandidentata	POGR	0.360	0.336	A	0.067	0.422	0.263	C	0.298	0.066	A	0.160	0.175	B	0.110	0.077	B
Populus	heterophylla	POHE	0.370	0.353	B	0.233	0.422	0.263	C	0.299	0.261	B	0.160	0.175	B	0.110	0.077	B
Populus	sargentii	POSA	0.370	0.353	B	0.233	0.422	0.263	C	0.299	0.261	B	0.160	0.175	B	0.110	0.077	B
Populus	species	POSP	0.370	0.370	A	0.067	0.422	0.263	C	0.300	0.066	A	0.160	0.027	A	0.110	0.027	A
Populus	tremuloides	POTR	0.350	0.353	B	0.233	0.422	0.263	C	0.299	0.261	B	0.160	0.175	B	0.110	0.077	B
Prosopis	species	PRSP	0.580	0.533	C	0.233	0.422	0.263	C	0.325	0.261	C	0.212	0.175	C	0.158	0.077	C
Prunus	americana	PRAM	0.470	0.489	B	0.080	0.418	0.065	B	0.281	0.261	B	0.212	0.175	C	0.158	0.077	C
Prunus	nigra	PRNI	0.470	0.489	B	0.080	0.418	0.065	B	0.281	0.261	B	0.212	0.175	C	0.158	0.077	C
Prunus	pensylvanica	PRPE	0.360	0.401	A	0.029	0.337	0.026	A	0.216	0.026	A	0.212	0.175	C	0.158	0.077	C
Prunus	serotina	PRSE	0.470	0.577	A	0.072	0.499	0.049	A	0.346	0.097	A	0.212	0.175	C	0.158	0.077	C
Prunus	species	PRSP2	0.470	0.489	B	0.080	0.418	0.065	B	0.281	0.261	B	0.212	0.175	C	0.158	0.077	C
Prunus	virginiana	PRVI	0.360	0.489	B	0.080	0.418	0.065	B	0.281	0.261	B	0.212	0.175	C	0.158	0.077	C
Pseudotsuga	menziesii	PSME	0.450	0.386	A	0.013	0.308	0.017	A	0.152	0.022	A	0.123	0.011	A	0.148	0.110	A
Quercus	agrifolia	QUAG	0.700	0.611	B	0.085	0.450	0.096	B	0.382	0.097	B	0.241	0.052	B	0.248	0.011	B
Quercus	alba	QUAL	0.600	0.567	A	0.031	0.387	0.019	A	0.335	0.045	A	0.168	0.071	A	0.248	0.011	B
Quercus	arizonica, grisea	QUAR	0.700	0.611	B	0.085	0.450	0.096	B	0.382	0.097	B	0.241	0.052	B	0.248	0.011	B
Quercus	bicolor	QUBI	0.640	0.611	B	0.085	0.450	0.096	B	0.382	0.097	B	0.241	0.052	B	0.248	0.011	B
Quercus	chrysolepis	QUCH	0.700	0.611	B	0.085	0.450	0.096	B	0.382	0.097	B	0.241	0.052	B	0.248	0.011	B
Quercus	coccinea	QUCO	0.600	0.571	A	0.053	0.502	0.041	A	0.442	0.033	A	0.241	0.052	B	0.248	0.011	B
Quercus	douglasii	QUDO	0.510	0.611	B	0.085	0.450	0.096	B	0.382	0.097	B	0.241	0.052	B	0.248	0.011	B
Quercus	durandii	QUDU	0.600	0.611	B	0.085	0.450	0.096	B	0.382	0.097	B	0.241	0.052	B	0.248	0.011	B
Quercus	ellipsoidalis	QUEL	0.560	0.611	B	0.085	0.450	0.096	B	0.382	0.097	B	0.241	0.052	B	0.248	0.011	B
Quercus	emoryi	QUEM	0.700	0.611	B	0.085	0.450	0.096	B	0.382	0.097	B	0.241	0.052	B	0.248	0.011	B
Quercus	engelmannii	QUEN	0.700	0.611	B	0.085	0.450	0.096	B	0.382	0.097	B	0.241	0.052	B	0.248	0.011	B
Quercus	falcata var. falcata	QUFA	0.520	0.611	B	0.085	0.450	0.096	B	0.382	0.097	B	0.241	0.052	B	0.248	0.011	B
Quercus	falcata var. pagodifolia	QUFA2	0.610	0.611	B	0.085	0.450	0.096	B	0.382	0.097	B	0.241	0.052	B	0.248	0.011	B
Quercus	gambelii	QUGA	0.640	0.611	B	0.085	0.450	0.096	B	0.382	0.097	B	0.241	0.052	B	0.248	0.011	B
Quercus	garryana	QUGA2	0.640	0.611	B	0.085	0.450	0.096	B	0.382	0.097	B	0.241	0.052	B	0.248	0.011	B
Quercus	hypoleucoides	QUHY	0.700	0.611	B	0.085	0.450	0.096	B	0.382	0.097	B	0.241	0.052	B	0.248	0.011	B
Quercus	ilicifolia	QUIL	0.560	0.611	B	0.085	0.450	0.096	B	0.382	0.097	B	0.241	0.052	B	0.248	0.011	B
Quercus	imbricaria	QUIM	0.560	0.611	B	0.085	0.450	0.096	B	0.382	0.097	B	0.241	0.052	B	0.248	0.011	B
Quercus	incana	QUIN	0.560	0.611	B	0.085	0.450	0.096	B	0.382	0.097	B	0.241	0.052	B	0.248	0.011	B
Quercus	kelloggii	QUKE	0.510	0.611	B	0.085	0.450	0.096	B	0.382	0.097	B	0.241	0.052	B	0.248	0.011	B
Quercus	laevis	QULA	0.520	0.611	B	0.085	0.450	0.096	B	0.382	0.097	B	0.241	0.052	B	0.248	0.011	B
Quercus	laurifolia	QULA2	0.560	0.611	B	0.085	0.450	0.096	B	0.382	0.097	B	0.241	0.052	B	0.248	0.011	B
Quercus	lobata	QULO	0.640	0.611	B	0.085	0.450	0.096	B	0.382	0.097	B	0.241	0.052	B	0.248	0.011	B
Quercus	lyrata	QULY	0.570	0.611	B	0.085	0.450	0.096	B	0.382	0.097	B	0.241	0.052	B	0.248	0.011	B
Quercus	macrocarpa	QUMA	0.580	0.611	B	0.085	0.450	0.096	B	0.382	0.097	B	0.241	0.052	B	0.248	0.011	B
Quercus	marilandica	QUMA2	0.560	0.611	B	0.085	0.450	0.096	B	0.382	0.097	B	0.241	0.052	B	0.248	0.011	B
Quercus	michauxii	QUMI	0.600	0.611	B	0.085	0.450	0.096	B	0.382	0.097	B	0.241	0.052	B	0.248	0.011	B
Quercus	muehlenbergii	QUMU	0.600	0.611	B	0.085	0.450	0.096	B	0.382	0.097	B	0.241	0.052	B	0.248	0.011	B
Quercus	nigra	QUNI	0.560	0.611	B	0.085	0.450	0.096	B	0.382	0.097	B	0.241	0.052	B	0.248	0.011	B
Quercus	nuttalli	QUNU	0.560	0.611	B	0.085	0.450	0.096	B	0.382	0.097	B	0.241	0.052	B	0.248	0.011	B

(Appendix 2 continued on next page)

(Appendix 2 continued)

Genus	Species	code	den0	den1	unc1	cod1	den2	unc2	cod2	den3	unc3	cod3	den4	unc4	cod4	den5	unc5	cod5
Quercus	oblongifolia	QUOB	0.700	0.611	0.085	B	0.450	0.096	B	0.382	0.097	B	0.241	0.052	B	0.248	0.011	B
Quercus	palustris	QUPA	0.580	0.611	0.085	B	0.450	0.096	B	0.382	0.097	B	0.241	0.052	B	0.248	0.011	B
Quercus	phellos	QUPH	0.560	0.611	0.085	B	0.450	0.096	B	0.382	0.097	B	0.241	0.052	B	0.248	0.011	B
Quercus	prinus	QUPR	0.570	0.729	0.078	A	0.489	0.093	A	0.294	0.042	A	0.241	0.052	B	0.248	0.011	B
Quercus	rubra	QURU	0.560	0.545	0.043	A	0.303	0.083	A	0.387	0.081	A	0.234	0.052	A	0.248	0.011	B
Quercus	shumardii	QUSH	0.560	0.611	0.085	B	0.450	0.096	B	0.382	0.097	B	0.241	0.052	B	0.248	0.011	B
Quercus	species	QUSP	0.580	0.565	0.019	A	0.462	0.039	A	0.318	0.043	A	0.196	0.020	A	0.248	0.021	A
Quercus	stellata	QUST	0.600	0.611	0.085	B	0.450	0.096	B	0.382	0.097	B	0.241	0.052	B	0.248	0.011	B
Quercus	velutina	QUVE	0.560	0.611	0.085	B	0.363	0.096	A	0.453	0.097	A	0.241	0.052	B	0.248	0.011	B
Quercus	virginiana	QUVI	0.800	0.611	0.085	B	0.450	0.096	B	0.382	0.097	B	0.241	0.052	B	0.248	0.011	B
Quercus	wislizeni	QUWI	0.700	0.611	0.085	B	0.450	0.096	B	0.382	0.097	B	0.241	0.052	B	0.248	0.011	B
Robinia	neomexicana	RONE	0.660	0.725	0.233	B	0.560	0.263	B	0.325	0.261	C	0.212	0.175	C	0.158	0.077	C
Robinia	pseudoacacia	ROPS	0.660	0.725	0.031	A	0.560	0.053	A	0.325	0.261	C	0.212	0.175	C	0.158	0.077	C
Salix	species	SASP	0.360	0.533	0.233	C	0.422	0.263	C	0.325	0.261	C	0.212	0.175	C	0.158	0.077	C
Sapium	sebiferum	SASE	0.470	0.533	0.233	C	0.422	0.263	C	0.325	0.261	C	0.212	0.175	C	0.158	0.077	C
Sassafras	albidum	SAAL	0.420	0.432	0.028	A	0.388	0.042	A	0.338	0.025	A	0.212	0.175	C	0.158	0.077	C
Sequoia	sempervirens	SESE	0.340	0.381	0.105	C	0.318	0.245	C	0.257	0.122	C	0.162	0.091	C	0.143	0.106	C
Sequoiadendron	giganteum	SEGI	0.340	0.381	0.105	C	0.318	0.245	C	0.257	0.122	C	0.162	0.091	C	0.143	0.106	C
Sorbus	americana	SOAM	0.420	0.533	0.233	C	0.422	0.263	C	0.325	0.261	C	0.212	0.175	C	0.158	0.077	C
Tamarix	species	TASP	0.400	0.533	0.233	C	0.422	0.263	C	0.325	0.261	C	0.212	0.175	C	0.158	0.077	C
Taxodium	distichum var. nutans	TADI	0.420	0.381	0.105	C	0.318	0.245	C	0.257	0.122	C	0.162	0.091	C	0.143	0.106	C
Taxus	brevifolia	TABR	0.600	0.381	0.105	C	0.318	0.245	C	0.257	0.122	C	0.162	0.091	C	0.143	0.106	C
Thuja	occidentalis	THOC	0.290	0.329	0.038	A	0.259	0.390	B	0.315	0.053	A	0.143	0.091	B	0.143	0.110	B
Thuja	plicata	THPL	0.310	0.318	0.038	A	0.259	0.390	A	0.248	0.030	A	0.132	0.002	A	0.143	0.110	A
Tilia	americana	TIAM	0.320	0.406	0.024	A	0.333	0.032	A	0.256	0.019	A	0.212	0.175	C	0.158	0.077	C
Tilia	heterophylla	TIHE	0.320	0.406	0.233	B	0.333	0.263	B	0.256	0.261	B	0.212	0.175	C	0.158	0.077	C
Tilia	species	TISP	0.320	0.406	0.233	B	0.333	0.263	B	0.256	0.261	B	0.212	0.175	C	0.158	0.077	C
Torreya	californica	TOCA	0.340	0.381	0.105	C	0.318	0.245	C	0.257	0.122	C	0.162	0.091	C	0.143	0.106	C
Tsuga	canadensis	TSCA	0.400	0.398	0.059	A	0.322	0.245	B	0.325	0.084	A	0.178	0.091	B	0.140	0.106	B
Tsuga	heterophylla	TSHE	0.420	0.399	0.022	A	0.346	0.023	A	0.258	0.019	A	0.166	0.025	A	0.108	0.106	A
Tsuga	mertensiana	TSME	0.420	0.380	0.059	B	0.322	0.245	B	0.282	0.122	B	0.178	0.091	B	0.140	0.106	B
Tsuga	species	TSSP	0.380	0.380	0.059	B	0.322	0.245	B	0.282	0.122	B	0.178	0.091	B	0.140	0.106	B
Ulmus	alata	ULAL	0.570	0.533	0.233	C	0.422	0.263	C	0.325	0.261	C	0.212	0.175	C	0.158	0.077	C
Ulmus	americana	ULAM	0.460	0.533	0.233	C	0.422	0.263	C	0.325	0.261	C	0.212	0.175	C	0.158	0.077	C
Ulmus	crassifolia	ULCR	0.570	0.533	0.233	C	0.422	0.263	C	0.325	0.261	C	0.212	0.175	C	0.158	0.077	C
Ulmus	pumila	ULPU	0.460	0.533	0.233	C	0.422	0.263	C	0.325	0.261	C	0.212	0.175	C	0.158	0.077	C
Ulmus	rubra	ULRU	0.480	0.533	0.233	C	0.422	0.263	C	0.325	0.261	C	0.212	0.175	C	0.158	0.077	C
Ulmus	serotina	ULSE	0.570	0.533	0.233	C	0.422	0.263	C	0.325	0.261	C	0.212	0.175	C	0.158	0.077	C
Ulmus	species	ULSP	0.500	0.533	0.233	C	0.422	0.263	C	0.325	0.261	C	0.212	0.175	C	0.158	0.077	C
Ulmus	thomasii	ULTH	0.570	0.533	0.233	C	0.422	0.263	C	0.325	0.261	C	0.212	0.175	C	0.158	0.077	C
Umbellularia	californica	UMCA	0.510	0.533	0.233	C	0.422	0.263	C	0.325	0.261	C	0.212	0.175	C	0.158	0.077	C
Vaccinium	arboreum	VAAR	0.470	0.533	0.233	C	0.422	0.263	C	0.325	0.261	C	0.212	0.175	C	0.158	0.077	C

CWD Density Predictions Metadata (Appendix 2)

Fieldname	Definition	Codes/units	Method
genus	Sample genus		
species	Sample species		
code	Genus-species code		
den0	Green density (decay class "0")	g/cm^3	
den1	Density of decay class 1	g/cm^3	
unc1	Uncertainty of den1	g/cm^3	
cod1	Uncertainty code for den1 (A, B, C)	A	Species sampled
		B	Genera sampled
		C	Species and genus not sampled
den2	Density of decay class 2	g/cm^3	
unc2	Uncertainty of den2	g/cm^3	
cod2	Uncertainty code for den2 (A, B, C)	A	Species sampled
		B	Genera sampled
		C	Species and genus not sampled
den3	Density of decay class 3	g/cm^3	
unc3	Uncertainty of den3	g/cm^3	
cod3	Uncertainty code for den3 (A, B, C)	A	Species sampled
		B	Genera sampled
		C	Species and genus not sampled
den4	Density of decay class 4	g/cm^3	
unc4	Uncertainty of den4	g/cm^3	
cod4	Uncertainty code for den4 (A, B, C)	A	Species sampled
		B	Genera sampled
		C	Species and genus not sampled
den5	Density of decay class 5	g/cm^3	
unc5	Uncertainty of den5	g/cm^3	
cod5	Uncertainty code for den5 (A, B, C)	A	Species sampled
		B	Genera sampled
		C	Species and genus not sampled

APPENDIX 3.—CWD relative density and its uncertainty for each decay class by species present in the U.S. FIA system

Genus	Species	code	den0	rel1	unc1	cod1	rel2	unc2	cod2	rel3	unc3	cod3	rel4	unc4	cod4	rel5	unc5	cod5
Abies	amabilis	ABAM	0.400	0.900	0.047	A	0.830	0.022	A	0.604	0.154	B	0.404	0.093	B	0.309	0.051	B
Abies	balsamea	ABBA	0.340	1.000	0.061	A	1.000	0.020	A	0.828	0.042	A	0.500	0.100	A	0.294	0.030	A
Abies	bracteata	ABBR	0.360	0.979	0.056	B	0.848	0.107	B	0.604	0.154	B	0.404	0.093	B	0.309	0.051	B
Abies	concolor	ABCO	0.370	0.958	0.019	A	0.759	0.018	A	0.470	0.014	A	0.381	0.016	A	0.330	0.020	A
Abies	fraseri	ABFR	0.340	0.979	0.056	B	0.848	0.107	B	0.604	0.154	B	0.404	0.093	B	0.309	0.051	B
Abies	grandis	ABGR	0.350	0.974	0.003	A	0.840	0.021	A	0.643	0.018	A	0.404	0.093	B	0.309	0.051	B
Abies	lasiocarpa	ABLA	0.310	1.000	0.028	A	0.929	0.078	A	0.752	0.023	A	0.490	0.030	A	0.377	0.011	A
Abies	magnifica	ABMA	0.360	1.000	0.013	A	0.939	0.053	A	0.471	0.019	A	0.329	0.014	A	0.233	0.010	A
Abies	magnifica var. shastensis	ABMA2	0.360	0.979	0.056	B	0.848	0.107	B	0.604	0.154	B	0.404	0.093	B	0.309	0.051	B
Abies	procera	ABPR	0.370	0.995	0.008	A	0.727	0.009	A	0.635	0.013	A	0.405	0.027	A	0.309	0.051	B
Abies	species	ABIE	0.340	0.979	0.056	B	0.848	0.107	B	0.604	0.154	B	0.438	0.093	A	0.309	0.051	B
Acacia	species	ACSP	0.600	0.944	0.136	C	0.734	0.270	C	0.583	0.265	C	0.370	0.180	C	0.282	0.094	C
Acer	barbatum	ACBA	0.540	0.941	0.036	B	0.709	0.270	B	0.533	0.265	B	0.317	0.180	B	0.241	0.094	B
Acer	glabrum	ACGL	0.440	0.941	0.036	B	0.709	0.270	B	0.533	0.265	B	0.317	0.180	B	0.241	0.094	B
Acer	grandidentatum	ACGR	0.440	0.941	0.036	B	0.709	0.270	B	0.533	0.265	B	0.317	0.180	B	0.241	0.094	B
Acer	macrophyllum	ACMA	0.440	0.941	0.036	B	0.709	0.270	B	0.533	0.265	B	0.317	0.180	B	0.241	0.094	B
Acer	negundo	ACNE	0.440	0.941	0.036	B	0.709	0.270	B	0.533	0.265	B	0.317	0.180	B	0.241	0.094	B
Acer	nigrum	ACNI	0.520	0.941	0.036	B	0.709	0.270	B	0.533	0.265	B	0.317	0.180	B	0.241	0.094	B
Acer	pensylvanicum	ACPE	0.440	0.941	0.036	B	0.709	0.270	B	0.533	0.265	B	0.317	0.180	B	0.241	0.094	B
Acer	rubrum	ACRU	0.490	0.963	0.050	A	0.716	0.064	A	0.583	0.075	A	0.317	0.180	B	0.241	0.094	B
Acer	saccharinum	ACSA2	0.440	0.941	0.036	B	0.709	0.270	B	0.533	0.265	B	0.317	0.180	B	0.241	0.094	B
Acer	saccharum	ACSA	0.560	0.919	0.028	A	0.705	0.063	A	0.496	0.043	A	0.317	0.014	A	0.241	0.015	A
Acer	species	ACSP2	0.600	0.941	0.036	B	0.709	0.270	B	0.533	0.265	B	0.317	0.180	B	0.241	0.094	B
Acer	spicatum	ACSP	0.440	0.941	0.036	B	0.709	0.270	B	0.533	0.265	B	0.317	0.180	B	0.241	0.094	B
Aesculus	californica	AECA	0.380	0.944	0.136	C	0.734	0.270	C	0.583	0.265	C	0.370	0.180	C	0.282	0.094	C
Aesculus	species	AESP	0.330	0.944	0.136	C	0.734	0.270	C	0.583	0.265	C	0.370	0.180	C	0.282	0.094	C
Ailanthus	altissima	AIAL	0.370	0.944	0.136	C	0.734	0.270	C	0.583	0.265	C	0.370	0.180	C	0.282	0.094	C
Aleurites	fordii	ALFO	0.470	0.944	0.136	C	0.734	0.270	C	0.583	0.265	C	0.370	0.180	C	0.282	0.094	C
Alnus	rubra	ALRU	0.370	0.990	0.008	A	0.836	0.047	A	0.505	0.011	A	0.277	0.008	A	0.300	0.049	A
Alnus	species	ALSP	0.370	0.990	0.136	B	0.836	0.270	B	0.505	0.265	B	0.277	0.180	B	0.300	0.094	B
Amelanchier	species	AMSP	0.660	0.944	0.136	C	0.734	0.270	C	0.583	0.265	C	0.370	0.180	C	0.282	0.094	C
Arbutus	menziesii	ARME	0.580	0.944	0.043	A	0.621	0.058	A	0.377	0.045	A	0.309	0.180	B	0.200	0.094	B
Asimina	triloba	ASTR	0.470	0.944	0.136	B	0.734	0.270	B	0.482	0.265	B	0.370	0.180	C	0.282	0.094	C
Betula	alleghaniensis	BEAL	0.550	0.992	0.008	B	0.836	0.047	B	0.505	0.030	A	0.283	0.020	A	0.183	0.010	A
Betula	lenta	BELE	0.600	1.000	0.069	A	0.700	0.099	A	0.472	0.085	B	0.309	0.180	B	0.200	0.094	B
Betula	lutea	BELU	0.600	1.000	0.043	A	0.621	0.058	A	0.377	0.045	A	0.309	0.180	B	0.200	0.094	B
Betula	nigra	BENI	0.560	0.992	0.136	B	0.660	0.270	B	0.482	0.265	B	0.309	0.180	B	0.200	0.094	B
Betula	occidentalis	BEOC	0.530	0.992	0.136	B	0.660	0.270	B	0.482	0.265	B	0.309	0.180	B	0.200	0.094	B
Betula	papyrifera	BEPA	0.480	0.977	0.052	A	0.660	0.270	A	0.733	0.128	A	0.309	0.180	A	0.200	0.094	A
Betula	papyrifera var. commutata	BEPA2	0.480	0.992	0.136	B	0.660	0.270	B	0.482	0.265	B	0.309	0.180	B	0.200	0.094	B
Betula	populifolia	BEPO	0.450	0.992	0.136	B	0.660	0.270	B	0.482	0.265	B	0.309	0.180	B	0.200	0.094	B
Betula	species	BESP	0.480	0.992	0.136	B	0.660	0.270	B	0.482	0.265	B	0.309	0.180	B	0.200	0.094	B

Genus	Species	code	den0	rel1	unc1	cod1	rel2	unc2	cod2	rel3	unc3	cod3	rel4	unc4	cod4	rel5	unc5	cod5
Brosimum	alcastrum	BRAL	0.740	0.836	0.010	A	0.491	0.052	A	0.335	0.053	A	0.193	0.018	A	0.270	0.094	A
Bumelia	lanuginosa	BULA	0.470	0.944	0.136	C	0.734	0.270	C	0.583	0.265	C	0.370	0.180	C	0.282	0.094	C
Bursera	simaruba	BUSI	0.330	0.973	0.026	A	0.643	0.029	A	0.387	0.017	A	0.385	0.060	A	0.352	0.094	A
Calocedrus	decurrens	CADE3	0.370	1.000	0.073	A	0.845	0.039	A	0.760	0.035	A	0.420	0.105	B	0.366	0.140	C
Carpinus	caroliniana	CACA	0.580	0.944	0.136	C	0.734	0.270	C	0.583	0.265	C	0.370	0.180	B	0.282	0.094	C
Carya	aquatica	CAAQ	0.610	0.950	0.072	B	0.653	0.085	B	0.381	0.075	A	0.279	0.180	B	0.244	0.094	B
Carya	cordiformis	CACO	0.600	1.000	0.074	A	0.612	0.074	A	0.415	0.050	A	0.279	0.180	B	0.244	0.094	B
Carya	glabra	CAGL	0.660	0.950	0.072	B	0.653	0.085	B	0.381	0.075	B	0.279	0.180	B	0.244	0.094	B
Carya	illinoensis	CAIL	0.600	0.950	0.072	B	0.653	0.085	B	0.381	0.075	B	0.279	0.180	B	0.244	0.094	B
Carya	laciniosa	CALA	0.620	0.950	0.072	B	0.653	0.085	B	0.381	0.075	B	0.279	0.180	B	0.244	0.094	B
Carya	myristicaeformis	CAMY	0.560	0.950	0.072	B	0.653	0.085	B	0.381	0.075	B	0.279	0.180	B	0.244	0.094	B
Carya	ovata	CAOV	0.640	0.861	0.071	A	0.748	0.087	A	0.481	0.065	A	0.279	0.180	B	0.244	0.094	B
Carya	species	CASP	0.620	1.000	0.031	A	0.673	0.021	A	0.315	0.017	A	0.279	0.027	A	0.244	0.059	A
Carya	texana	CATE	0.540	0.950	0.072	B	0.653	0.085	B	0.381	0.075	B	0.279	0.180	B	0.244	0.094	B
Carya	tomentosa	CATO	0.640	0.939	0.059	A	0.581	0.033	A	0.313	0.075	A	0.279	0.180	B	0.244	0.094	B
Castanea	dentata	CADE	0.400	0.900	0.046	A	0.870	0.038	A	0.630	0.056	A	0.370	0.180	C	0.366	0.094	C
Castanea	ozarkensis	CAOZ	0.400	0.900	0.136	B	0.870	0.270	B	0.638	0.265	B	0.370	0.180	C	0.282	0.094	C
Castanea	pumila	CAPU	0.400	0.900	0.136	B	0.870	0.270	B	0.638	0.265	B	0.370	0.180	C	0.282	0.094	C
Castanopsis	species	CAST	0.420	0.944	0.136	C	0.734	0.270	C	0.583	0.265	C	0.370	0.180	C	0.282	0.094	C
Catalpa	species	CATA	0.380	0.944	0.136	C	0.734	0.270	C	0.583	0.265	C	0.370	0.180	C	0.282	0.094	C
Cecropia	obtusifolia	CEOB	0.300	0.900	0.048	A	0.687	0.049	A	0.460	0.023	A	0.320	0.034	A	0.282	0.094	C
Celtis	laevigata	CELA	0.470	0.944	0.136	C	0.734	0.270	C	0.583	0.265	C	0.370	0.180	C	0.282	0.094	C
Celtis	occidentalis	CEOC	0.490	0.944	0.136	C	0.734	0.270	C	0.583	0.265	C	0.370	0.180	C	0.282	0.094	C
Celtis	species	CESP	0.490	0.944	0.136	C	0.734	0.270	C	0.583	0.265	C	0.370	0.180	C	0.282	0.094	C
Cercis	canadensis	CECA	0.580	0.944	0.136	C	0.734	0.270	C	0.583	0.265	C	0.370	0.180	C	0.282	0.094	C
Cercocarpus	intricatus	CEIN	1.000	0.944	0.136	C	0.734	0.270	C	0.583	0.265	C	0.370	0.180	C	0.282	0.094	C
Cercocarpus	ledifolius	CELE	1.000	0.944	0.136	C	0.734	0.270	C	0.583	0.265	C	0.370	0.180	C	0.282	0.094	C
Cercocarpus	montanus	CEMO	1.000	0.944	0.136	C	0.734	0.270	C	0.583	0.265	C	0.370	0.180	C	0.282	0.094	C
Chamaecyparis	lawsoniana	CHLA	0.390	0.956	0.073	C	0.827	0.314	C	0.678	0.201	C	0.426	0.105	C	0.366	0.140	C
Chamaecyparis	nootkatensis	CHNO	0.420	0.956	0.073	C	0.827	0.314	C	0.678	0.201	C	0.426	0.105	C	0.366	0.140	C
Chamaecyparis	thyoides	CHTH	0.310	0.956	0.073	C	0.827	0.314	C	0.678	0.201	C	0.426	0.105	C	0.366	0.140	C
Cladrastis	lutea	CLLU	0.520	0.944	0.136	C	0.734	0.270	C	0.583	0.265	C	0.370	0.180	C	0.282	0.094	C
Cornus	florida	COFL	0.640	0.944	0.136	C	0.734	0.270	C	0.583	0.265	C	0.370	0.180	C	0.282	0.094	C
Cornus	nuttallii	CONU	0.580	0.944	0.136	C	0.734	0.270	C	0.583	0.265	C	0.370	0.180	C	0.282	0.094	C
Cornus	species	COSP	0.640	0.944	0.136	C	0.734	0.270	C	0.583	0.265	C	0.370	0.180	C	0.282	0.094	C
Cotinus	obovatus	COOB	0.470	0.944	0.136	C	0.734	0.270	C	0.583	0.265	C	0.370	0.180	C	0.282	0.094	C
Crataegus	species	CRSP	0.620	0.944	0.136	C	0.734	0.270	C	0.583	0.265	C	0.370	0.180	C	0.282	0.094	C
Cupressus	species	CUSP	0.440	0.956	0.073	C	0.827	0.314	C	0.678	0.201	C	0.426	0.105	C	0.366	0.140	C
Diospyros	virginiana	DIVI	0.640	0.944	0.136	C	0.734	0.270	C	0.583	0.265	C	0.370	0.180	C	0.282	0.094	C
Eucalyptus	species	EUSP	0.670	0.944	0.136	C	0.734	0.270	C	0.583	0.265	C	0.370	0.180	C	0.282	0.094	C
Fagus	grandifolia	FAGR	0.560	0.976	0.056	A	0.614	0.042	A	0.479	0.032	A	0.375	0.028	A	0.250	0.012	A
Fraxinus	americana	FRAM	0.550	0.864	0.070	A	0.520	0.070	A	0.570	0.048	A	0.370	0.180	C	0.182	0.030	A
Fraxinus	latifolia	FRLA	0.500	0.864	0.136	B	0.576	0.270	B	0.542	0.265	B	0.370	0.180	C	0.182	0.094	B
Fraxinus	nigra	FRNI	0.450	0.864	0.136	B	0.576	0.270	B	0.542	0.265	B	0.370	0.180	C	0.182	0.094	B

(Appendix 3 continued on next page)

(Appendix 3 continued)

Genus	Species	code	den0	rel1	unc1	cod1	rel2	unc2	cod2	rel3	unc3	cod3	rel4	unc4	cod4	rel5	unc5	cod5
Fraxinus	pennsylvanica	FRPE	0.530	0.864	0.136	B	0.576	0.270	B	0.542	0.265	B	0.370	0.180	C	0.182	0.094	B
Fraxinus	profunda	FRPR	0.540	0.864	0.136	B	0.576	0.270	B	0.542	0.265	B	0.370	0.180	C	0.182	0.094	B
Fraxinus	quadrangulata	FRQU	0.530	0.864	0.136	B	0.576	0.270	B	0.542	0.265	B	0.370	0.180	C	0.182	0.094	B
Fraxinus	species	FRSP	0.540	0.864	0.136	B	0.576	0.270	B	0.542	0.265	B	0.370	0.180	C	0.182	0.094	B
Gleditsia	aquatica	GLAQ	0.600	0.944	0.136	C	0.734	0.270	C	0.583	0.265	C	0.370	0.180	C	0.282	0.094	C
Gleditsia	triacanthos	GLTR	0.600	0.944	0.136	C	0.734	0.270	C	0.583	0.265	C	0.370	0.180	C	0.282	0.094	C
Gordonia	lasianthus	GOLA	0.370	0.944	0.136	C	0.734	0.270	C	0.583	0.265	C	0.370	0.180	C	0.282	0.094	C
Gymnocladus	dioicus	GYDI	0.500	0.944	0.136	C	0.734	0.270	C	0.583	0.265	C	0.370	0.180	C	0.282	0.094	C
Halesia	species	HASP	0.320	0.944	0.136	C	0.734	0.270	C	0.583	0.265	C	0.370	0.180	C	0.282	0.094	C
Heliocarpos	appendiculatus	HEAP	0.250	0.716	0.041	A	0.604	0.035	A	0.536	0.008	A	0.452	0.020	A	0.282	0.094	C
Ilex	opaca	ILOP	0.500	0.944	0.136	C	0.734	0.270	C	0.583	0.265	C	0.370	0.180	C	0.282	0.094	C
Juglans	cinerea	JUCI	0.360	0.944	0.136	C	0.734	0.270	C	0.583	0.265	C	0.370	0.180	C	0.282	0.094	C
Juglans	species	JUSP	0.510	0.944	0.136	C	0.734	0.270	C	0.583	0.265	C	0.370	0.180	C	0.282	0.094	C
Juglans	nigra	JUNI	0.510	0.944	0.136	C	0.734	0.270	C	0.583	0.265	C	0.370	0.180	C	0.282	0.094	C
Juniperus	monosperma	JUMO	0.450	0.956	0.073	C	0.827	0.314	C	0.678	0.201	C	0.426	0.105	C	0.366	0.140	C
Juniperus	occidentalis	JUOC	0.440	0.956	0.073	C	0.827	0.314	C	0.678	0.201	C	0.426	0.105	C	0.366	0.140	C
Juniperus	species	JUSP2	0.440	0.944	0.136	C	0.734	0.270	C	0.583	0.265	C	0.370	0.180	C	0.282	0.094	C
Larix	laricina	LALA	0.490	0.956	0.073	C	0.827	0.314	C	0.678	0.201	C	0.426	0.105	C	0.366	0.140	C
Larix	lyallii	LALY	0.480	0.956	0.073	C	0.827	0.314	C	0.678	0.201	C	0.426	0.105	C	0.366	0.140	C
Larix	occidentalis	LAOC	0.480	0.956	0.073	C	0.827	0.314	C	0.678	0.201	C	0.426	0.105	C	0.366	0.140	C
Larix	species	LASP	0.440	0.956	0.073	C	0.827	0.314	C	0.678	0.201	C	0.426	0.105	C	0.366	0.140	C
Liquidambar	styraciflua	LIST	0.460	0.978	0.008	A	0.720	0.031	A	0.496	0.025	A	0.370	0.180	A	0.282	0.094	C
Liriodendron	tulipifera	LITU	0.400	0.940	0.042	A	0.786	0.041	A	0.523	0.026	A	0.353	0.055	A	0.282	0.094	C
Lithocarpus	densiflorus	LIDE	0.580	0.944	0.136	C	0.734	0.270	C	0.583	0.265	C	0.370	0.180	C	0.282	0.094	C
Maclura	pomifera	MAPO	0.760	0.944	0.136	C	0.734	0.270	C	0.583	0.265	C	0.370	0.180	C	0.282	0.094	C
Magnolia	acuminata	MAAC	0.450	0.850	0.028	A	0.798	0.084	A	0.500	0.059	A	0.370	0.180	A	0.282	0.094	C
Magnolia	species	MASP	0.450	0.850	0.136	B	0.798	0.270	B	0.500	0.265	B	0.370	0.180	B	0.282	0.094	C
Malus	species	MASP2	0.610	0.944	0.136	C	0.734	0.270	C	0.583	0.265	C	0.370	0.180	C	0.282	0.094	C
Manilkara	zapota	MAZA	0.950	0.790	0.040	A	0.787	0.040	A	0.740	0.138	A	0.566	0.050	A	0.282	0.094	C
Melia	azedarach	MEAZ	0.470	0.944	0.136	C	0.734	0.270	C	0.583	0.265	C	0.370	0.180	C	0.282	0.094	C
Morus	alba	MOAL	0.590	0.944	0.136	C	0.734	0.270	C	0.583	0.265	C	0.370	0.180	C	0.282	0.094	C
Morus	rubra	MORU	0.590	0.944	0.136	C	0.734	0.270	C	0.583	0.265	C	0.370	0.180	C	0.282	0.094	C
Morus	species	MOSP	0.590	0.944	0.136	C	0.734	0.270	C	0.583	0.265	C	0.370	0.180	C	0.282	0.094	C
Myrcianthes	fragans	MYFR	0.750	0.968	0.136	A	0.872	0.047	A	0.745	0.095	A	0.400	0.180	A	0.282	0.094	C
Nyssa	aquatica	NYAQ	0.460	0.944	0.136	C	0.734	0.270	C	0.583	0.265	C	0.370	0.180	C	0.282	0.094	C
Nyssa	ogeche	NYOG	0.460	0.944	0.136	C	0.734	0.270	C	0.583	0.265	C	0.370	0.180	C	0.282	0.094	C
Nyssa	sylvatica	NYSY	0.460	0.944	0.136	C	0.734	0.270	C	0.583	0.265	C	0.370	0.180	C	0.282	0.094	C
Olneya	tesota	OLTE	1.000	0.944	0.136	C	0.734	0.270	C	0.583	0.265	C	0.370	0.180	C	0.282	0.094	C
Ostrya	virginiana	OSVI	0.630	0.944	0.136	C	0.734	0.270	C	0.583	0.265	C	0.370	0.180	C	0.282	0.094	C
Oxydendrum	arboreum	OXAR	0.500	1.000	0.103	A	0.812	0.034	A	0.674	0.057	A	0.370	0.180	A	0.282	0.094	C
Paulownia	tomentosa	PATO	0.380	0.944	0.136	C	0.734	0.270	C	0.583	0.265	C	0.370	0.180	C	0.282	0.094	C
Persea	borbonia	PEBO	0.510	0.944	0.136	C	0.734	0.270	C	0.583	0.265	C	0.370	0.180	C	0.282	0.094	C
Picea	abies	PIAB	0.380	0.998	0.073	B	0.858	0.314	B	0.745	0.201	B	0.426	0.105	B	0.347	0.140	B
Picea	breweriana	PIBR	0.330	0.998	0.073	B	0.858	0.314	B	0.745	0.201	B	0.426	0.105	B	0.347	0.140	B

Genus	Species	code	den0	rel1	unc1	cod1	rel2	unc2	cod2	rel3	unc3	cod3	rel4	unc4	cod4	rel5	unc5	cod5
Picea	*engelmannii*	PIEN	0.330	0.916	0.073	B	0.782	0.023	A	0.745	0.201	B	0.355	0.026	A	0.347	0.140	B
Picea	*glauca*	PIGL	0.410	0.998	0.073	B	0.858	0.314	B	0.745	0.201	B	0.426	0.105	B	0.347	0.140	B
Picea	*lutzii*	PILU	0.370	0.989	0.034	A	0.913	0.035	A	0.671	0.067	A	0.397	0.027	A	0.271	0.018	A
Picea	*mariana*	PIMA	0.380	0.998	0.073	B	0.858	0.314	B	0.745	0.201	B	0.426	0.105	B	0.347	0.140	B
Picea	*pungens*	PIPU	0.380	0.998	0.073	B	0.858	0.314	B	0.745	0.201	B	0.426	0.105	B	0.347	0.140	B
Picea	*rubens*	PIRU	0.380	1.000	0.057	A	0.858	0.314	B	0.832	0.112	A	0.426	0.029	A	0.347	0.140	A
Picea	*sitchensis*	PISI	0.370	1.000	0.008	A	0.868	0.021	A	0.740	0.021	A	0.476	0.029	A	0.385	0.008	A
Picea	*species*	PICE	0.380	0.998	0.073	B	0.858	0.314	B	0.745	0.201	B	0.426	0.105	B	0.347	0.140	B
Pinus	*albicaulis*	PIAL	0.370	0.916	0.061	B	0.826	0.090	B	0.697	0.106	B	0.421	0.063	B	0.407	0.124	B
Pinus	*aristata*	PIAR	0.370	0.916	0.061	B	0.826	0.090	B	0.697	0.106	B	0.421	0.063	B	0.407	0.124	B
Pinus	*arizonica*	PIAR2	0.370	0.916	0.061	B	0.826	0.090	B	0.697	0.106	B	0.421	0.063	B	0.407	0.124	B
Pinus	*attenuata*	PIAT	0.370	0.916	0.061	B	0.826	0.090	B	0.697	0.106	B	0.421	0.063	B	0.407	0.124	B
Pinus	*balfouriana*	PIBA	0.370	0.916	0.061	B	0.826	0.090	B	0.697	0.106	B	0.421	0.063	B	0.407	0.124	B
Pinus	*banksiana*	PIBA2	0.400	0.916	0.061	B	0.826	0.090	B	0.697	0.106	B	0.421	0.063	B	0.407	0.124	B
Pinus	*clausa*	PICL	0.460	0.916	0.061	B	0.826	0.090	B	0.697	0.106	B	0.421	0.063	B	0.407	0.124	B
Pinus	*contorta*	PICO	0.380	0.977	0.020	A	0.956	0.013	A	0.809	0.022	A	0.512	0.019	A	0.432	0.009	A
Pinus	*coulteri*	PICO2	0.370	0.916	0.061	B	0.826	0.090	B	0.697	0.106	B	0.421	0.063	B	0.407	0.124	B
Pinus	*discolor*	PIDI	0.500	0.916	0.061	B	0.826	0.090	B	0.697	0.106	B	0.421	0.063	B	0.407	0.124	B
Pinus	*echinata*	PIEC	0.470	0.916	0.061	B	0.826	0.090	B	0.697	0.106	B	0.421	0.063	B	0.407	0.124	B
Pinus	*edulis*	PIED	0.500	0.916	0.061	B	0.826	0.090	B	0.697	0.106	B	0.421	0.063	B	0.407	0.124	B
Pinus	*elliottii*	PIEL	0.540	0.916	0.061	B	0.826	0.090	B	0.697	0.106	B	0.421	0.063	B	0.407	0.124	B
Pinus	*engelmannii*	PIEN2	0.370	0.916	0.061	B	0.826	0.090	B	0.745	0.096	B	0.421	0.063	B	0.347	0.038	B
Pinus	*flexilis*	PIFL	0.370	0.916	0.061	B	0.826	0.090	B	0.697	0.106	B	0.421	0.063	B	0.407	0.124	B
Pinus	*glabra*	PIGL2	0.370	0.998	0.061	B	0.858	0.090	B	0.745	0.106	B	0.426	0.063	B	0.347	0.124	B
Pinus	*jefferyi*	PIJE	0.370	0.869	0.026	A	0.835	0.042	A	0.664	0.047	A	0.454	0.039	A	0.407	0.124	A
Pinus	*lambertiana*	PILA	0.340	1.000	0.037	A	0.788	0.011	A	0.553	0.020	A	0.364	0.025	A	0.407	0.124	A
Pinus	*leiophylla*	PILE	0.370	0.916	0.061	B	0.826	0.090	B	0.697	0.106	B	0.421	0.063	B	0.407	0.124	B
Pinus	*monophylla*	PIMO	0.500	0.916	0.061	B	0.826	0.090	B	0.697	0.106	B	0.421	0.063	B	0.407	0.124	B
Pinus	*monticola*	PIMO3	0.350	0.983	0.005	A	0.866	0.012	A	0.880	0.015	A	0.421	0.063	B	0.407	0.124	B
Pinus	*muricata*	PIMU	0.370	0.916	0.061	B	0.826	0.090	B	0.697	0.106	B	0.421	0.063	B	0.407	0.124	B
Pinus	*nigra*	PINI	0.410	0.916	0.061	B	0.826	0.090	B	0.697	0.106	B	0.421	0.063	B	0.407	0.124	B
Pinus	*palustris*	PIPA	0.540	0.916	0.061	B	0.826	0.090	B	0.697	0.106	B	0.421	0.063	B	0.407	0.124	B
Pinus	*ponderosa*	PIPO	0.380	0.889	0.005	A	0.876	0.018	A	0.868	0.035	A	0.339	0.008	A	0.495	0.134	A
Pinus	*pungens*	PIPU2	0.490	0.998	0.061	B	0.858	0.090	B	0.745	0.106	B	0.426	0.063	B	0.347	0.124	B
Pinus	*radiata*	PIRA	0.370	0.916	0.061	B	0.826	0.090	B	0.697	0.106	B	0.421	0.063	B	0.407	0.124	B
Pinus	*resinosa*	PIRE	0.410	0.829	0.061	A	0.826	0.090	B	0.659	0.106	A	0.366	0.063	A	0.268	0.124	A
Pinus	*rigida*	PIRI	0.470	0.916	0.061	B	0.826	0.090	B	0.697	0.106	B	0.421	0.063	B	0.407	0.124	B
Pinus	*sabiniana*	PISA	0.370	0.916	0.061	B	0.826	0.090	B	0.697	0.106	B	0.421	0.063	B	0.407	0.124	B
Pinus	*serotina*	PISE	0.510	0.916	0.061	B	0.826	0.090	B	0.697	0.106	B	0.421	0.063	B	0.407	0.124	B
Pinus	*strobiformis*	PIST2	0.350	0.916	0.061	B	0.826	0.090	B	0.697	0.106	B	0.421	0.063	B	0.407	0.124	B
Pinus	*strobus*	PIST	0.340	0.916	0.061	B	0.826	0.090	B	0.697	0.106	B	0.421	0.063	B	0.407	0.124	B
Pinus	*sylvestris*	PISY	0.410	0.916	0.061	B	0.826	0.090	B	0.697	0.106	B	0.421	0.063	B	0.407	0.124	B
Pinus	*taeda*	PITA	0.470	0.829	0.012	A	0.682	0.005	A	0.550	0.002	A	0.423	0.004	A	0.421	0.124	A
Pinus	*virginiana*	PIVI	0.450	0.916	0.061	B	0.826	0.090	B	0.697	0.106	B	0.421	0.063	B	0.407	0.124	B

(Appendix 3 continued on next page)

(Appendix 3 continued)

Genus	Species	code	den0	rel1	unc1	cod1	rel2	unc2	cod2	rel3	unc3	cod3	rel4	unc4	cod4	rel5	unc5	cod5
Planera	aquatica	PLAQ	0.530	0.944	0.136	C	0.734	0.270	C	0.583	0.265	C	0.370	0.180	C	0.282	0.094	C
Platanus	occidentalis	PLOC	0.460	0.944	0.136	C	0.734	0.270	C	0.583	0.265	C	0.370	0.180	C	0.282	0.094	C
Populus	alba	POAL	0.370	0.967	0.136	B	0.734	0.270	C	0.819	0.265	B	0.432	0.180	B	0.297	0.094	B
Populus	angustifolia	POAN	0.340	0.967	0.136	B	0.734	0.270	C	0.819	0.265	B	0.432	0.180	B	0.297	0.094	B
Populus	balsamifera	POBA	0.310	0.967	0.136	B	0.734	0.270	C	0.819	0.265	B	0.432	0.180	B	0.297	0.094	B
Populus	deltoides	PODE	0.370	0.967	0.136	B	0.734	0.270	C	0.819	0.265	B	0.432	0.180	B	0.297	0.094	B
Populus	fremontii	POFR	0.340	0.967	0.136	B	0.734	0.270	C	0.819	0.265	A	0.432	0.180	B	0.297	0.094	B
Populus	grandidentata	POGR	0.360	0.933	0.067	A	0.734	0.270	C	0.828	0.066	A	0.432	0.180	B	0.297	0.094	B
Populus	heterophylla	POHE	0.370	0.967	0.136	B	0.734	0.270	C	0.819	0.265	B	0.432	0.180	B	0.297	0.094	B
Populus	sargentii	POSA	0.370	0.967	0.136	B	0.734	0.270	C	0.819	0.265	B	0.432	0.180	B	0.297	0.094	B
Populus	species	POSP	0.370	1.000	0.136	A	0.734	0.270	C	0.811	0.265	A	0.432	0.180	A	0.297	0.094	A
Populus	tremuloides	POTR	0.350	0.967	0.136	B	0.734	0.270	C	0.819	0.265	B	0.432	0.180	B	0.297	0.094	B
Prosopis	species	PRSP	0.580	0.944	0.136	C	0.734	0.270	C	0.583	0.265	C	0.370	0.180	C	0.282	0.094	C
Prunus	americana	PRAM	0.470	1.000	0.136	B	0.968	0.270	B	0.668	0.265	B	0.370	0.180	C	0.282	0.094	C
Prunus	nigra	PRNI	0.470	1.000	0.136	B	0.968	0.270	A	0.668	0.265	B	0.370	0.180	C	0.282	0.094	C
Prunus	pensylvanica	PRPE	0.360	1.000	0.029	A	0.936	0.026	A	0.600	0.026	A	0.370	0.180	C	0.282	0.094	C
Prunus	serotina	PRSE	0.470	1.000	0.072	A	1.000	0.049	A	0.736	0.097	A	0.370	0.180	C	0.282	0.094	C
Prunus	species	PRSP2	0.470	1.000	0.136	B	0.968	0.270	B	0.668	0.265	B	0.370	0.180	C	0.282	0.094	C
Prunus	virginiana	PRVI	0.360	1.000	0.136	B	0.968	0.270	B	0.668	0.265	B	0.370	0.180	C	0.282	0.094	C
Pseudotsuga	menziesii	PSME	0.450	0.858	0.013	A	0.723	0.017	A	0.444	0.022	A	0.305	0.011	A	0.329	0.110	A
Quercus	agrifolia	QUAG	0.700	0.981	0.051	B	0.779	0.099	B	0.665	0.114	B	0.416	0.086	B	0.428	0.011	B
Quercus	alba	QUAL	0.600	0.973	0.031	A	0.746	0.019	A	0.558	0.045	A	0.280	0.071	A	0.428	0.011	B
Quercus	arizonica, grisea	QUAR	0.700	0.981	0.051	B	0.779	0.099	B	0.665	0.114	B	0.416	0.086	B	0.428	0.011	B
Quercus	bicolor	QUBI	0.640	0.981	0.051	B	0.779	0.099	B	0.665	0.114	B	0.416	0.086	B	0.428	0.011	B
Quercus	chrysolepis	QUCH	0.700	0.981	0.051	B	0.779	0.099	B	0.665	0.114	B	0.416	0.086	B	0.428	0.011	B
Quercus	coccinea	QUCO	0.600	0.952	0.053	A	0.837	0.041	A	0.737	0.033	A	0.416	0.086	B	0.428	0.011	B
Quercus	douglasii	QUDO	0.510	0.981	0.051	B	0.779	0.099	B	0.665	0.114	B	0.416	0.086	B	0.428	0.011	B
Quercus	durandii	QUDU	0.600	0.981	0.051	B	0.779	0.099	B	0.665	0.114	B	0.416	0.086	B	0.428	0.011	B
Quercus	ellipsoidalis	QUEL	0.560	0.981	0.051	B	0.779	0.099	B	0.665	0.114	B	0.416	0.086	B	0.428	0.011	B
Quercus	emoryi	QUEM	0.700	0.981	0.051	B	0.779	0.099	B	0.665	0.114	B	0.416	0.086	B	0.428	0.011	B
Quercus	engelmannii	QUEN	0.700	0.981	0.051	B	0.779	0.099	B	0.665	0.114	B	0.416	0.086	B	0.428	0.011	B
Quercus	falcata var. falcata	QUFA2	0.520	0.981	0.051	B	0.779	0.099	B	0.665	0.114	B	0.416	0.086	B	0.428	0.011	B
Quercus	falcata var. pagodaefolia	QUFA2	0.610	0.981	0.051	B	0.779	0.099	B	0.665	0.114	B	0.416	0.086	B	0.428	0.011	B
Quercus	gambelii	QUGA	0.640	0.981	0.051	B	0.779	0.099	B	0.665	0.114	B	0.416	0.086	B	0.428	0.011	B
Quercus	garryana	QUGA2	0.640	0.981	0.051	B	0.779	0.099	B	0.665	0.114	B	0.416	0.086	B	0.428	0.011	B
Quercus	hypoleucoides	QUHY	0.700	0.981	0.051	B	0.779	0.099	B	0.665	0.114	B	0.416	0.086	B	0.428	0.011	B
Quercus	ilicifolia	QUIL	0.560	0.981	0.051	B	0.779	0.099	B	0.665	0.114	B	0.416	0.086	B	0.428	0.011	B
Quercus	imbricaria	QUIM	0.560	0.981	0.051	B	0.779	0.099	B	0.665	0.114	B	0.416	0.086	B	0.428	0.011	B
Quercus	incana	QUIN	0.560	0.981	0.051	B	0.779	0.099	B	0.665	0.114	B	0.416	0.086	B	0.428	0.011	B
Quercus	kelloggii	QUKE	0.510	0.981	0.051	B	0.779	0.099	B	0.665	0.114	B	0.416	0.086	B	0.428	0.011	B
Quercus	laevis	QULA	0.520	0.981	0.051	B	0.779	0.099	B	0.665	0.114	B	0.416	0.086	B	0.428	0.011	B
Quercus	laurifolia	QULA2	0.560	0.981	0.051	B	0.779	0.099	B	0.665	0.114	B	0.416	0.086	B	0.428	0.011	B
Quercus	lobata	QULO	0.640	0.981	0.051	B	0.779	0.099	B	0.665	0.114	B	0.416	0.086	B	0.428	0.011	B
Quercus	lyrata	QULY	0.570	0.981	0.051	B	0.779	0.099	B	0.665	0.114	B	0.416	0.086	B	0.428	0.011	B

Genus	Species	code	den0	rel1	unc1	cod1	rel2	unc2	cod2	rel3	unc3	cod3	rel4	unc4	cod4	rel5	unc5	cod5
Quercus	macrocarpa	QUMA	0.580	0.981	0.051	B	0.779	0.099	B	0.665	0.114	B	0.416	0.086	B	0.428	0.011	B
Quercus	marilandica	QUMA2	0.560	0.981	0.051	B	0.779	0.099	B	0.665	0.114	B	0.416	0.086	B	0.428	0.011	B
Quercus	michauxii	QUMI	0.600	0.981	0.051	B	0.779	0.099	B	0.665	0.114	B	0.416	0.086	B	0.428	0.011	B
Quercus	muehlenbergii	QUMU	0.600	0.981	0.051	B	0.779	0.099	B	0.665	0.114	B	0.416	0.086	B	0.428	0.011	B
Quercus	nigra	QUNI	0.560	0.981	0.051	B	0.779	0.099	B	0.665	0.114	B	0.416	0.086	B	0.428	0.011	B
Quercus	nuttallii	QUNU	0.560	0.981	0.051	B	0.779	0.099	B	0.665	0.114	B	0.416	0.086	B	0.428	0.011	B
Quercus	oblongifolia	QUOB	0.700	0.981	0.051	B	0.779	0.099	B	0.665	0.114	B	0.416	0.086	B	0.428	0.011	B
Quercus	palustris	QUPA	0.580	0.981	0.051	B	0.779	0.099	B	0.665	0.114	B	0.416	0.086	B	0.428	0.011	B
Quercus	phellos	QUPH	0.560	0.981	0.051	B	0.779	0.099	B	0.665	0.114	B	0.416	0.086	B	0.428	0.011	B
Quercus	prinus	QUPR	0.570	1.000	0.078	A	0.858	0.093	A	0.516	0.042	A	0.416	0.086	B	0.428	0.011	B
Quercus	rubra	QURU	0.560	0.991	0.043	A	0.795	0.083	A	0.690	0.081	A	0.416	0.086	B	0.428	0.011	B
Quercus	shumardii	QUSH	0.560	0.981	0.051	B	0.779	0.099	B	0.665	0.114	B	0.416	0.086	B	0.428	0.011	B
Quercus	species	QUSP	0.580	0.974	0.019	A	0.797	0.039	A	0.649	0.043	A	0.483	0.020	A	0.428	0.021	A
Quercus	stellata	QUST	0.600	0.981	0.051	B	0.779	0.099	B	0.665	0.114	B	0.416	0.086	B	0.428	0.011	B
Quercus	velutina	QUVE	0.560	0.981	0.051	B	0.648	0.099	A	0.809	0.114	A	0.416	0.086	B	0.428	0.011	B
Quercus	virginiana	QUVI	0.800	0.981	0.051	B	0.779	0.099	B	0.665	0.114	B	0.416	0.086	B	0.428	0.011	B
Quercus	wislizeni	QUWI	0.700	0.981	0.051	B	0.779	0.099	B	0.665	0.114	B	0.416	0.086	B	0.428	0.011	B
Robinia	neomexicana	RONE	0.660	1.000	0.136	B	0.848	0.270	B	0.583	0.265	C	0.370	0.180	C	0.282	0.094	C
Robinia	pseudoacacia	ROPS	0.660	1.000	0.031	A	0.848	0.053	A	0.583	0.265	C	0.370	0.180	C	0.282	0.094	C
Sabal	species	SASP	0.550	0.927	0.082	A	0.744	0.091	A	0.615	0.074	A	0.265	0.112	A	0.282	0.094	C
Salix	species	SASP	0.360	0.944	0.136	C	0.734	0.270	C	0.583	0.265	C	0.370	0.180	C	0.282	0.094	C
Sapium	sebiferum	SASE	0.470	0.944	0.136	C	0.734	0.270	C	0.583	0.265	C	0.370	0.180	C	0.282	0.094	C
Sassafras	albidum	SAAL	0.420	1.000	0.028	A	0.924	0.042	A	0.805	0.025	A	0.426	0.105	C	0.282	0.140	C
Sequoia	sempervirens	SESE	0.340	0.956	0.073	C	0.827	0.314	C	0.678	0.201	C	0.426	0.105	C	0.366	0.140	C
Sequoiadendron	giganteum	SEGI	0.340	0.956	0.073	C	0.827	0.314	C	0.678	0.201	C	0.426	0.105	C	0.366	0.140	C
Sorbus	americana	SOAM	0.420	0.944	0.136	C	0.734	0.270	C	0.583	0.265	C	0.370	0.180	C	0.282	0.094	C
Tamarix	species	TASP	0.400	0.944	0.136	C	0.734	0.270	C	0.583	0.265	C	0.370	0.180	C	0.282	0.094	C
Taxodium	distichum var. nutans	TADI	0.420	0.956	0.073	C	0.827	0.314	C	0.678	0.201	C	0.426	0.105	C	0.366	0.140	C
Taxus	brevifolia	TABR	0.600	0.956	0.073	C	0.827	0.314	C	0.678	0.201	C	0.426	0.105	C	0.366	0.140	C
Thuja	occidentalis	THOC	0.290	1.000	0.038	A	0.835	0.195	B	1.000	0.053	A	0.461	0.001	B	0.461	0.055	B
Thuja	plicata	THPL	0.310	1.000	0.073	A	0.835	0.390	A	0.800	0.030	A	0.462	0.002	A	0.461	0.110	A
Tilia	americana	TIAM	0.320	1.000	0.024	A	1.000	0.032	A	0.800	0.019	A	0.370	0.180	C	0.282	0.094	C
Tilia	heterophylla	TIHE	0.320	1.000	0.136	B	1.000	0.270	B	0.800	0.265	B	0.370	0.180	C	0.282	0.094	C
Tilia	species	TISP	0.320	1.000	0.136	B	1.000	0.270	B	0.800	0.265	B	0.370	0.180	C	0.282	0.094	C
Torreya	californica	TOCA	0.340	0.956	0.073	C	0.827	0.314	C	0.678	0.201	C	0.426	0.105	C	0.366	0.140	C
Tsuga	canadensis	TSCA	0.400	0.995	0.059	A	0.767	0.314	B	0.813	0.084	B	0.425	0.105	B	0.333	0.140	B
Tsuga	heterophylla	TSHE	0.420	0.890	0.022	A	0.767	0.023	A	0.636	0.019	A	0.425	0.025	A	0.332	0.106	A
Tsuga	mertensiana	TSME	0.420	0.916	0.056	B	0.767	0.314	B	0.681	0.086	B	0.425	0.105	B	0.333	0.140	B
Tsuga	species	TSSP	0.380	0.916	0.056	B	0.767	0.314	B	0.681	0.086	B	0.425	0.105	B	0.333	0.140	B
Ulmus	alata	ULAL	0.570	0.944	0.136	C	0.734	0.270	C	0.583	0.265	C	0.370	0.180	C	0.282	0.094	C
Ulmus	americana	ULAM	0.460	0.944	0.136	C	0.734	0.270	C	0.583	0.265	C	0.370	0.180	C	0.282	0.094	C
Ulmus	crassifolia	ULCR	0.570	0.944	0.136	C	0.734	0.270	C	0.583	0.265	C	0.370	0.180	C	0.282	0.094	C
Ulmus	pumila	ULPU	0.460	0.944	0.136	C	0.734	0.270	C	0.583	0.265	C	0.370	0.180	C	0.282	0.094	C
Ulmus	rubra	ULRU	0.480	0.944	0.136	C	0.734	0.270	C	0.583	0.265	C	0.370	0.180	C	0.282	0.094	C

(Appendix 3 continued on next page)

(Appendix 3 continued)

Genus	Species	code	den0	rel1	unc1	cod1	rel2	unc2	cod2	rel3	unc3	cod3	rel4	unc4	cod4	rel5	unc5	cod5
Ulmus	serotina	ULSE	0.570	0.944	0.136	C	0.734	0.270	C	0.583	0.265	C	0.370	0.180	C	0.282	0.094	C
Ulmus	species	ULSP	0.500	0.944	0.136	C	0.734	0.270	C	0.583	0.265	C	0.370	0.180	C	0.282	0.094	C
Ulmus	thomasii	ULTH	0.570	0.944	0.136	C	0.734	0.270	C	0.583	0.265	C	0.370	0.180	C	0.282	0.094	C
Umbellularia	californica	UMCA	0.510	0.944	0.136	C	0.734	0.270	C	0.583	0.265	C	0.370	0.180	C	0.282	0.094	C
Vaccinium	arboreum	VAAR	0.470	0.944	0.136	C	0.734	0.270	C	0.583	0.265	C	0.370	0.180	C	0.282	0.094	C

CWD Relative Density Predictions Metadata (Appendix 3)

Fieldname	Definition	Code/units	Method
genus	genus		
species	species		
code	genus-species code		
den0	green density	g/cm^3	
unc0	uncertainty green density		
rel1	relative density decay class 1	dimensionless	
unc1	uncertainty of rel1	dimensionless	
cod1	uncertainty code for rel1	A	Species sampled
		B	Genera sampled
		C	Species and genus not sampled
rel2	relative density decay class 2	dimensionless	
unc2	uncertainty of rel2	dimensionless	
cod2	uncertainty code for rel2	A	Species sampled
		B	Genera sampled
		C	Species and genus not sampled
rel3	relative density decay class 3	dimensionless	
unc3	uncertainty of rel3	dimensionless	
cod3	uncertainty code for rel3	A	Species sampled
		B	Genera sampled
		C	Species and genus not sampled
rel4	relative density decay class 4	dimensionless	
unc4	uncertainty of rel4	dimensionless	
cod4	uncertainty code for rel4	A	Species sampled
		B	Genera sampled
		C	Species and genus not sampled
rel5	relative density decay class 5	dimensionless	
unc5	uncertainty of rel5	dimensionless	
cod5	uncertainty code for rel5	A	Species sampled
		B	Genera sampled
		C	Species and genus not sampled

Appendix 4.—FWD absolute and relative density and their uncertainty for each size class by species present in the U.S. FIA system

Species code	Size class	Bole init density	Branch-bole ratio	Uncert B-B ratio	Uncert_bb ratio code	FWD initial density	Uncert FWD density	Uncert FWD code	Relative density	Uncert Rel density	Uncert Rel Den code	Decayed density	Uncert Decayed density	Uncert Decayed code
ABAM	1	0.40	1.29	0.02	B	0.51	0.01	A	0.82	0.19	C	0.42	0.04	C
ABAM	2	0.40	1.38	0.02	A	0.55	0.01	A	0.96	0.01	A	0.53	0.01	A
ABAM	3	0.40	1.12	0.03	A	0.45	0.01	A	0.99	0.03	A	0.44	0.01	A
ABAM	4	0.40	1.35	0.01	B	0.54	0.00	A	0.80	0.12	C	0.43	0.06	C
ABBA	1	0.34	2.04	0.09	B	0.70	0.03	A	0.64	0.06	B	0.45	0.04	B
ABBA	2	0.34	1.19	0.21	A	0.41	0.03	A	1.00	0.01	A	0.41	0.04	B
ABBA	3	0.34	1.11	0.23	C	0.38	0.08	B	1.00	0.09	B	0.38	0.04	B
ABBA	4	0.34	1.25	0.17	C	0.43	0.06	B	0.80	0.12	C	0.34	0.06	C
ABBR	1	0.36	1.47	0.31	C	0.53	0.11	B	0.82	0.19	C	0.44	0.07	C
ABBR	2	0.36	1.22	0.18	C	0.44	0.07	B	1.03	0.13	C	0.45	0.04	C
ABBR	3	0.36	1.11	0.23	C	0.40	0.08	B	0.95	0.12	C	0.38	0.05	C
ABBR	4	0.36	1.25	0.17	C	0.45	0.06	B	0.80	0.12	C	0.36	0.06	C
ABCO	1	0.37	1.47	0.31	C	0.54	0.11	B	0.82	0.19	C	0.44	0.07	C
ABCO	2	0.37	1.22	0.18	C	0.45	0.07	B	1.03	0.13	C	0.46	0.04	C
ABCO	3	0.37	1.11	0.23	C	0.41	0.08	B	0.95	0.12	C	0.39	0.05	C
ABCO	4	0.37	1.25	0.17	C	0.46	0.06	B	0.80	0.12	C	0.37	0.06	C
ABFR	1	0.34	1.47	0.31	C	0.50	0.10	B	0.82	0.19	C	0.41	0.07	C
ABFR	2	0.34	1.22	0.18	C	0.41	0.06	B	1.03	0.13	C	0.42	0.04	C
ABFR	3	0.34	1.11	0.23	C	0.38	0.08	B	0.95	0.12	C	0.36	0.04	C
ABFR	4	0.34	1.25	0.17	C	0.43	0.06	B	0.80	0.12	C	0.34	0.06	C
ABGR	1	0.35	1.47	0.31	C	0.51	0.11	B	1.14	0.11	B	0.58	0.05	B
ABGR	2	0.35	1.22	0.18	C	0.43	0.06	B	1.16	0.11	B	0.50	0.05	B
ABGR	3	0.35	1.11	0.23	C	0.39	0.08	B	0.95	0.12	C	0.37	0.04	C
ABGR	4	0.35	1.25	0.17	C	0.44	0.06	B	0.80	0.12	C	0.35	0.06	C
ABLA	1	0.31	2.02	0.05	B	0.63	0.02	A	0.65	0.06	B	0.41	0.04	B
ABLA	2	0.31	1.38	0.04	B	0.43	0.01	A	1.03	0.13	C	0.44	0.03	C
ABLA	3	0.31	1.21	0.03	B	0.38	0.01	A	0.95	0.12	C	0.36	0.03	C
ABLA	4	0.31	1.50	0.05	B	0.47	0.02	A	0.85	0.08	B	0.40	0.04	B
ABMA	1	0.36	1.47	0.31	C	0.53	0.11	B	0.82	0.19	C	0.44	0.07	C
ABMA	2	0.36	1.22	0.18	C	0.44	0.07	B	1.03	0.13	C	0.45	0.04	C
ABMA	3	0.36	1.11	0.23	C	0.40	0.08	B	0.95	0.12	C	0.38	0.05	C
ABMA	4	0.36	1.25	0.17	C	0.45	0.06	B	0.80	0.12	C	0.36	0.06	C
ABMA2	1	0.36	1.47	0.31	C	0.53	0.11	B	0.82	0.19	C	0.44	0.07	C
ABMA2	2	0.36	1.22	0.18	C	0.44	0.07	B	1.03	0.13	C	0.45	0.04	C
ABMA2	3	0.36	1.11	0.23	C	0.40	0.08	B	0.95	0.12	C	0.38	0.05	C
ABMA2	4	0.36	1.25	0.17	C	0.45	0.06	B	0.80	0.12	C	0.36	0.06	C
ABPR	1	0.37	1.47	0.31	C	0.54	0.11	B	0.82	0.19	C	0.44	0.07	C
ABPR	2	0.37	1.22	0.18	C	0.45	0.07	B	1.03	0.13	C	0.46	0.04	C
ABPR	3	0.37	1.11	0.23	C	0.41	0.08	B	0.95	0.12	C	0.39	0.05	C
ABPR	4	0.37	1.25	0.17	C	0.46	0.06	B	0.80	0.12	C	0.37	0.06	C

Species code	Size class	Bole init density	Branch-bole ratio	Uncert B-B ratio	Uncert_bb ratio code	FWD initial density	Uncert FWD density	Uncert FWD code	Relative density	Uncert Rel density	Uncert Rel Den code	Decayed density	Uncert Decayed density	Uncert Decayed code
ABIE	1	0.34	1.47	0.31	C	0.50	0.10	B	0.82	0.19	C	0.41	0.07	C
ABIE	2	0.34	1.22	0.18	C	0.41	0.06	B	1.03	0.13	C	0.42	0.04	C
ABIE	3	0.34	1.11	0.23	C	0.38	0.08	B	0.95	0.12	C	0.36	0.04	C
ABIE	4	0.34	1.25	0.17	C	0.43	0.06	B	0.80	0.12	C	0.34	0.06	C
ACSP2	1	0.60	1.47	0.31	C	0.88	0.18	B	0.83	0.15	C	0.73	0.16	C
ACSP2	2	0.60	1.22	0.18	C	0.73	0.11	B	0.85	0.14	C	0.62	0.09	C
ACSP2	3	0.60	1.11	0.23	C	0.66	0.14	B	0.92	0.12	C	0.61	0.10	C
ACSP2	4	0.60	1.25	0.17	C	0.75	0.10	B	0.71	0.12	C	0.54	0.09	C
ACBA	1	0.54	1.47	0.31	C	0.79	0.16	B	0.83	0.10	C	0.65	0.13	C
ACBA	2	0.54	1.22	0.18	C	0.66	0.10	B	0.85	0.15	C	0.56	0.07	C
ACBA	3	0.54	1.11	0.23	C	0.60	0.12	B	0.92	0.14	C	0.55	0.08	C
ACBA	4	0.54	1.25	0.17	C	0.68	0.09	B	0.71	0.12	C	0.49	0.07	C
ACGL	1	0.44	1.47	0.31	C	0.65	0.13	B	0.83	0.10	C	0.54	0.09	C
ACGL	2	0.44	1.22	0.18	C	0.54	0.08	B	0.85	0.15	C	0.46	0.05	C
ACGL	3	0.44	1.11	0.23	C	0.49	0.10	B	0.92	0.14	C	0.45	0.06	C
ACGL	4	0.44	1.25	0.17	C	0.55	0.08	B	0.71	0.12	C	0.39	0.06	C
ACGR	1	0.44	1.47	0.31	C	0.65	0.13	B	0.83	0.10	C	0.54	0.09	C
ACGR	2	0.44	1.22	0.18	C	0.54	0.08	B	0.85	0.15	C	0.46	0.05	C
ACGR	3	0.44	1.11	0.23	C	0.49	0.10	B	0.92	0.14	C	0.45	0.06	C
ACGR	4	0.44	1.25	0.17	C	0.55	0.08	B	0.71	0.12	C	0.39	0.06	C
ACMA	1	0.44	0.96	0.01	B	0.42	0.01	A	0.83	0.10	C	0.35	0.03	C
ACMA	2	0.44	1.13	0.01	B	0.50	0.00	A	0.85	0.15	C	0.43	0.03	C
ACMA	3	0.44	1.05	0.01	B	0.46	0.01	A	0.92	0.14	C	0.42	0.04	C
ACMA	4	0.44	1.07	0.01	B	0.47	0.00	A	0.71	0.12	C	0.34	0.04	C
ACNE	1	0.44	1.47	0.31	C	0.65	0.13	B	0.83	0.10	C	0.54	0.09	C
ACNE	2	0.44	1.22	0.18	C	0.54	0.08	B	0.85	0.15	C	0.46	0.05	C
ACNE	3	0.44	1.11	0.23	C	0.49	0.10	B	0.92	0.14	C	0.45	0.06	C
ACNE	4	0.44	1.25	0.17	C	0.55	0.08	B	0.71	0.12	C	0.39	0.06	C
ACNI	1	0.52	1.47	0.31	C	0.76	0.16	B	0.83	0.10	C	0.63	0.13	C
ACNI	2	0.52	1.22	0.18	C	0.63	0.10	B	0.85	0.15	C	0.54	0.07	C
ACNI	3	0.52	1.11	0.23	C	0.58	0.12	B	0.92	0.14	C	0.53	0.08	C
ACNI	4	0.52	1.25	0.17	C	0.65	0.09	B	0.71	0.12	C	0.46	0.07	C
ACPE	1	0.44	1.47	0.31	C	0.65	0.13	B	0.83	0.10	C	0.54	0.09	C
ACPE	2	0.44	1.22	0.18	C	0.54	0.08	B	0.85	0.15	C	0.46	0.05	C
ACPE	3	0.44	1.11	0.23	C	0.49	0.10	B	0.92	0.14	C	0.45	0.06	C
ACPE	4	0.44	1.25	0.17	C	0.55	0.08	B	0.71	0.12	C	0.39	0.06	C
ACRU	1	0.49	1.19	0.03	B	0.58	0.02	A	0.83	0.10	C	0.48	0.03	C
ACRU	2	0.49	1.13	0.01	B	0.55	0.01	A	0.85	0.15	C	0.47	0.03	C
ACRU	3	0.49	1.03	0.02	B	0.51	0.01	A	0.92	0.14	C	0.47	0.04	C
ACRU	4	0.49	1.12	0.01	B	0.55	0.01	A	0.71	0.12	C	0.39	0.04	C
ACSA2	1	0.44	1.47	0.31	C	0.65	0.13	B	0.83	0.10	C	0.54	0.09	C

(Appendix 4 continued on next page)

Species code	Size class	Bole init density	Branch-bole ratio	Uncert B-B ratio	Uncert_ bb ratio code	FWD initial density	Uncert FWD density	Uncert FWD code	Relative density	Uncert Rel density	Uncert Rel Den code	Decayed density	Uncert Decayed density	Uncert Decayed code
ACSA2	2	0.44	1.22	0.18	C	0.54	0.08	B	0.85	0.15	C	0.46	0.05	C
ACSA2	3	0.44	1.11	0.23	C	0.49	0.10	B	0.92	0.14	C	0.45	0.06	C
ACSA2	4	0.44	1.25	0.17	C	0.55	0.08	B	0.71	0.12	C	0.39	0.06	C
ACSA	1	0.56	1.47	0.31	C	0.82	0.17	B	0.83	0.10	C	0.68	0.14	C
ACSA	2	0.56	1.22	0.18	C	0.68	0.10	B	0.85	0.15	C	0.58	0.07	C
ACSA	3	0.56	1.11	0.23	C	0.62	0.13	B	0.92	0.14	C	0.57	0.09	C
ACSA	4	0.56	1.25	0.17	C	0.70	0.10	B	0.71	0.12	C	0.50	0.08	C
ACER	1	0.49	1.47	0.31	C	0.72	0.15	B	0.83	0.10	C	0.60	0.11	C
ACER	2	0.49	1.22	0.18	C	0.60	0.09	B	0.85	0.15	C	0.51	0.06	C
ACER	3	0.49	1.11	0.23	C	0.54	0.11	B	0.92	0.14	C	0.50	0.07	C
ACER	4	0.49	1.25	0.17	C	0.61	0.08	B	0.71	0.12	C	0.44	0.07	C
ACSP	1	0.44	1.47	0.31	C	0.65	0.13	B	0.83	0.10	C	0.54	0.09	C
ACSP	2	0.44	1.22	0.18	C	0.54	0.08	B	0.87	0.05	B	0.47	0.03	B
ACSP	3	0.44	1.11	0.23	C	0.49	0.10	B	0.92	0.14	C	0.45	0.06	C
ACSP	4	0.44	1.25	0.17	C	0.55	0.08	B	0.81	0.07	B	0.44	0.04	B
AECA	1	0.38	1.47	0.31	C	0.56	0.12	B	0.83	0.10	C	0.46	0.07	C
AECA	2	0.38	1.22	0.18	C	0.46	0.07	B	0.85	0.15	C	0.39	0.04	C
AECA	3	0.38	1.11	0.23	C	0.42	0.09	B	0.92	0.14	C	0.39	0.05	C
AECA	4	0.38	1.25	0.17	C	0.48	0.07	B	0.71	0.12	C	0.34	0.05	C
AESP	1	0.33	1.47	0.31	C	0.49	0.10	B	0.83	0.10	C	0.41	0.06	C
AESP	2	0.33	1.22	0.18	C	0.40	0.06	B	0.85	0.15	C	0.34	0.04	C
AESP	3	0.33	1.11	0.23	C	0.37	0.08	B	0.92	0.14	C	0.34	0.05	C
AESP	4	0.33	1.25	0.17	C	0.41	0.06	B	0.71	0.12	C	0.29	0.05	C
AIAL	1	0.37	1.47	0.31	C	0.54	0.11	B	0.83	0.10	C	0.45	0.07	C
AIAL	2	0.37	1.22	0.18	C	0.45	0.07	B	0.85	0.15	C	0.38	0.04	C
AIAL	3	0.37	1.11	0.23	C	0.41	0.08	B	0.92	0.14	C	0.38	0.05	C
AIAL	4	0.37	1.25	0.17	C	0.46	0.06	B	0.71	0.12	C	0.33	0.05	C
ALFO	1	0.47	1.47	0.31	C	0.69	0.14	B	0.83	0.10	C	0.57	0.10	C
ALFO	2	0.47	1.22	0.18	C	0.57	0.09	B	0.85	0.15	C	0.49	0.06	C
ALFO	3	0.47	1.11	0.23	C	0.52	0.11	B	0.92	0.14	C	0.48	0.07	C
ALFO	4	0.47	1.25	0.17	C	0.59	0.08	B	0.71	0.12	C	0.42	0.06	C
ALRU	1	0.40	1.86	0.03	B	0.74	0.01	A	0.83	0.10	C	0.61	0.03	C
ALRU	2	0.40	1.27	0.01	B	0.51	0.00	A	0.85	0.15	C	0.43	0.03	C
ALRU	3	0.40	1.15	0.01	B	0.46	0.00	A	0.92	0.14	C	0.42	0.03	C
ALRU	4	0.40	1.39	0.02	B	0.56	0.01	A	0.71	0.12	C	0.40	0.04	C
ALSP	1	0.37	1.47	0.31	C	0.54	0.11	B	0.83	0.10	C	0.45	0.07	C
ALSP	2	0.37	1.22	0.18	C	0.45	0.07	B	0.85	0.15	C	0.38	0.04	C
ALSP	3	0.37	1.11	0.23	C	0.41	0.08	B	0.92	0.14	C	0.38	0.05	C
ALSP	4	0.37	1.25	0.17	C	0.46	0.06	B	0.71	0.12	C	0.33	0.05	C
ALTE	1	0.40	1.27	0.03	B	0.51	0.01	A	0.83	0.10	C	0.42	0.03	C
ALTE	2	0.40	0.97	0.02	B	0.39	0.01	A	0.85	0.15	C	0.33	0.03	C

Species code	Size class	Bole init density	Branch-bole ratio	Uncert B-B ratio	Uncert_bb ratio code	FWD initial density	Uncert FWD density	Uncert FWD code	Relative density	Uncert Rel density	Uncert Rel Den code	Decayed density	Uncert Decayed density	Uncert Decayed code
ALTE	3	0.40	1.11	0.23	C	0.44	0.09	B	0.92	0.14	C	0.40	0.05	C
ALTE	4	0.40	1.07	0.03	B	0.43	0.01	A	0.71	0.12	C	0.31	0.04	C
AMSP	1	0.66	1.47	0.31	C	0.97	0.20	B	0.83	0.10	C	0.80	0.20	C
AMSP	2	0.66	1.22	0.18	C	0.80	0.12	B	0.85	0.15	C	0.68	0.10	C
AMSP	3	0.66	1.11	0.23	C	0.73	0.15	B	0.92	0.14	C	0.67	0.11	C
AMSP	4	0.66	1.25	0.17	C	0.83	0.11	B	0.71	0.12	C	0.59	0.10	C
ARME	1	0.58	1.47	0.31	C	0.85	0.18	B	0.83	0.10	C	0.70	0.16	C
ARME	2	0.58	1.22	0.18	C	0.71	0.11	B	0.85	0.15	C	0.61	0.08	C
ARME	3	0.58	1.11	0.23	C	0.64	0.13	B	0.92	0.14	C	0.59	0.09	C
ARME	4	0.58	1.25	0.17	C	0.73	0.10	B	0.71	0.12	C	0.52	0.08	C
ASTR	1	0.47	1.47	0.31	C	0.69	0.14	B	0.83	0.10	C	0.57	0.10	C
ASTR	2	0.47	1.22	0.18	C	0.57	0.09	B	0.85	0.15	C	0.49	0.06	C
ASTR	3	0.47	1.11	0.23	C	0.52	0.11	B	0.92	0.14	C	0.48	0.07	C
ASTR	4	0.47	1.25	0.17	C	0.59	0.08	B	0.71	0.12	C	0.42	0.06	C
BEAL	1	0.55	1.47	0.31	C	0.81	0.17	B	0.83	0.10	C	0.67	0.14	C
BEAL	2	0.55	1.22	0.18	C	0.67	0.10	B	0.85	0.15	C	0.57	0.07	C
BEAL	3	0.55	1.11	0.23	C	0.61	0.13	B	0.92	0.14	C	0.56	0.09	C
BEAL	4	0.55	1.25	0.17	C	0.69	0.10	B	0.71	0.12	C	0.49	0.08	C
BELE	1	0.60	1.47	0.31	C	0.88	0.18	B	0.83	0.10	C	0.73	0.16	C
BELE	2	0.60	1.22	0.18	C	0.73	0.11	B	0.85	0.15	C	0.62	0.09	C
BELE	3	0.60	1.11	0.23	C	0.66	0.14	B	0.92	0.14	C	0.61	0.10	C
BELE	4	0.60	1.25	0.17	C	0.75	0.10	B	0.71	0.12	C	0.54	0.09	C
BENI	1	0.56	1.47	0.31	C	0.82	0.17	B	0.83	0.10	C	0.68	0.14	C
BENI	2	0.56	1.22	0.18	C	0.68	0.10	B	0.85	0.15	C	0.58	0.07	C
BENI	3	0.56	1.11	0.23	C	0.62	0.13	B	0.92	0.14	C	0.57	0.09	C
BENI	4	0.56	1.25	0.17	C	0.70	0.10	B	0.71	0.12	C	0.50	0.08	C
BEOC	1	0.53	1.47	0.31	C	0.78	0.16	B	0.83	0.10	C	0.65	0.13	C
BEOC	2	0.53	1.22	0.18	C	0.65	0.10	B	0.85	0.15	C	0.55	0.07	C
BEOC	3	0.53	1.11	0.23	C	0.59	0.12	B	0.92	0.14	C	0.54	0.08	C
BEOC	4	0.53	1.25	0.17	C	0.66	0.09	B	0.71	0.12	C	0.47	0.07	C
BEPA	1	0.48	1.43	0.04	B	0.69	0.02	A	0.83	0.10	C	0.57	0.03	C
BEPA	2	0.48	1.07	0.05	A	0.52	0.01	A	0.85	0.15	C	0.44	0.03	C
BEPA	3	0.48	1.11	0.23	C	0.53	0.11	B	0.92	0.14	C	0.49	0.07	C
BEPA	4	0.48	1.25	0.17	C	0.60	0.08	B	0.71	0.12	C	0.43	0.06	C
BEPAC	1	0.48	1.47	0.31	C	0.71	0.15	B	0.83	0.10	C	0.59	0.11	C
BEPAC	2	0.48	1.22	0.18	C	0.58	0.09	B	0.85	0.15	C	0.49	0.06	C
BEPAC	3	0.48	1.11	0.23	C	0.53	0.11	B	0.92	0.14	C	0.49	0.07	C
BEPAC	4	0.48	1.25	0.17	C	0.60	0.08	B	0.71	0.12	C	0.43	0.06	C
BEPO	1	0.45	1.47	0.31	C	0.66	0.14	B	0.83	0.10	C	0.55	0.10	C
BEPO	2	0.45	1.22	0.18	C	0.55	0.08	B	0.85	0.15	C	0.47	0.05	C
BEPO	3	0.45	1.11	0.23	C	0.50	0.10	B	0.92	0.14	C	0.46	0.06	C

(Appendix 4 continued on next page)

(Appendix 4 continued)

Species code	Size class	Bole init density	Branch-bole ratio	Uncert B-B ratio	Uncert_bb ratio code	FWD initial density	Uncert FWD density	Uncert FWD code	Relative density	Uncert Rel density	Uncert Rel Den code	Decayed density	Uncert Decayed density	Uncert Decayed code
BEPO	4	0.45	1.25	0.17	C	0.56	0.08	B	0.71	0.12	C	0.40	0.06	C
BESP	1	0.48	1.47	0.31	C	0.71	0.15	B	0.83	0.10	C	0.59	0.11	C
BESP	2	0.48	1.22	0.18	C	0.58	0.09	B	0.68	0.04	B	0.40	0.03	A
BESP	3	0.48	1.11	0.23	C	0.53	0.11	B	0.92	0.14	C	0.49	0.07	C
BESP	4	0.48	1.25	0.17	C	0.60	0.08	B	0.63	0.08	B	0.38	0.05	A
BEPL	1	0.45	1.47	0.31	C	0.66	0.14	B	0.83	0.10	C	0.55	0.10	C
BEPL	2	0.45	0.40	0.02	B	0.18	0.01	A	0.85	0.15	C	0.15	0.03	C
BEPL	3	0.45	1.11	0.23	C	0.50	0.10	B	0.92	0.14	C	0.46	0.06	C
BEPL	4	0.45	0.40	0.02	B	0.18	0.01	A	0.71	0.12	C	0.13	0.04	C
BULA	1	0.47	1.47	0.31	C	0.69	0.14	B	0.83	0.10	C	0.57	0.10	C
BULA	2	0.47	1.22	0.18	C	0.57	0.09	B	0.85	0.15	C	0.49	0.06	C
BULA	3	0.47	1.11	0.23	C	0.52	0.11	B	0.92	0.14	C	0.48	0.07	C
BULA	4	0.47	1.25	0.17	C	0.59	0.08	B	0.71	0.12	C	0.42	0.06	C
CADE3	1	0.37	1.47	0.31	C	0.54	0.11	B	0.82	0.19	C	0.44	0.07	C
CADE3	2	0.37	1.22	0.18	C	0.45	0.07	B	1.03	0.13	C	0.46	0.04	C
CADE3	3	0.37	1.11	0.23	C	0.41	0.08	B	0.95	0.12	C	0.39	0.05	C
CADE3	4	0.37	1.25	0.17	C	0.46	0.06	B	0.80	0.12	C	0.37	0.06	C
CACA	1	0.58	1.47	0.31	C	0.85	0.18	B	0.83	0.10	C	0.70	0.16	C
CACA	2	0.58	1.22	0.18	C	0.71	0.11	B	0.85	0.15	C	0.61	0.08	C
CACA	3	0.58	1.11	0.23	C	0.64	0.13	B	0.92	0.14	C	0.59	0.09	C
CACA	4	0.58	1.25	0.17	C	0.73	0.10	B	0.71	0.12	C	0.52	0.08	C
CAAQ	1	0.61	1.47	0.31	C	0.90	0.19	B	0.83	0.10	C	0.75	0.17	C
CAAQ	2	0.61	1.22	0.18	C	0.74	0.11	B	0.85	0.15	C	0.63	0.09	C
CAAQ	3	0.61	1.11	0.23	C	0.68	0.14	B	0.92	0.14	C	0.62	0.10	C
CAAQ	4	0.61	1.25	0.17	C	0.76	0.11	B	0.71	0.12	C	0.54	0.09	C
CACO	1	0.60	1.47	0.31	C	0.88	0.18	B	0.83	0.10	C	0.73	0.16	C
CACO	2	0.60	1.22	0.18	C	0.73	0.11	B	0.85	0.15	C	0.62	0.09	C
CACO	3	0.60	1.11	0.23	C	0.66	0.14	B	0.92	0.14	C	0.61	0.09	C
CACO	4	0.60	1.25	0.17	C	0.75	0.10	B	0.71	0.12	C	0.54	0.09	C
CAGL	1	0.66	1.47	0.31	C	0.97	0.20	B	0.83	0.10	C	0.80	0.20	C
CAGL	2	0.66	1.22	0.18	C	0.80	0.12	B	0.85	0.15	C	0.68	0.10	C
CAGL	3	0.66	1.11	0.23	C	0.73	0.15	B	0.92	0.14	C	0.67	0.11	C
CAGL	4	0.66	1.25	0.17	C	0.83	0.11	B	0.71	0.12	C	0.59	0.10	C
CAIL	1	0.60	1.47	0.31	C	0.88	0.18	B	0.83	0.10	C	0.73	0.16	C
CAIL	2	0.60	1.22	0.18	C	0.73	0.11	B	0.85	0.15	C	0.62	0.09	C
CAIL	3	0.60	1.11	0.23	C	0.66	0.14	B	0.92	0.14	C	0.61	0.10	C
CAIL	4	0.60	1.25	0.17	C	0.75	0.10	B	0.71	0.12	C	0.54	0.09	C
CALA	1	0.62	1.47	0.31	C	0.91	0.19	B	0.83	0.10	C	0.75	0.18	C
CALA	2	0.62	1.22	0.18	C	0.76	0.11	B	0.85	0.15	C	0.65	0.09	C
CALA	3	0.62	1.11	0.23	C	0.69	0.14	B	0.92	0.14	C	0.63	0.10	C
CALA	4	0.62	1.25	0.17	C	0.78	0.11	B	0.71	0.12	C	0.56	0.10	C

Species code	Size class	Bole init density	Branch-bole ratio	Uncert B-B ratio	Uncert_bb ratio code	FWD initial density	Uncert FWD density	Uncert FWD code	Relative density	Uncert Rel density	Uncert Rel Den code	Decayed density	Uncert Decayed density	Uncert Decayed code
CAMY	1	0.56	1.47	0.31	C	0.82	0.17	B	0.83	0.10	C	0.68	0.14	C
CAMY	2	0.56	1.22	0.18	C	0.68	0.10	B	0.85	0.15	C	0.58	0.07	C
CAMY	3	0.56	1.11	0.23	C	0.62	0.13	B	0.92	0.14	C	0.57	0.09	C
CAMY	4	0.56	1.25	0.17	C	0.70	0.10	B	0.71	0.12	C	0.50	0.08	C
CAOV	1	0.64	1.47	0.31	C	0.94	0.20	B	0.83	0.10	C	0.78	0.19	C
CAOV	2	0.64	1.22	0.18	C	0.78	0.12	B	0.85	0.15	C	0.66	0.10	C
CAOV	3	0.64	1.11	0.23	C	0.71	0.15	B	0.92	0.14	C	0.65	0.11	C
CAOV	4	0.64	1.25	0.17	C	0.80	0.11	B	0.71	0.12	C	0.57	0.10	C
CASP	1	0.62	1.47	0.31	C	0.91	0.19	B	0.83	0.10	C	0.75	0.18	C
CASP	2	0.62	1.22	0.18	C	0.76	0.11	B	0.85	0.15	C	0.65	0.09	C
CASP	3	0.62	1.11	0.23	C	0.69	0.14	B	0.92	0.14	C	0.63	0.10	C
CASP	4	0.62	1.25	0.17	C	0.78	0.11	B	0.71	0.12	C	0.56	0.10	C
CATE	1	0.54	1.47	0.31	C	0.79	0.16	B	0.83	0.10	C	0.65	0.13	C
CATE	2	0.54	1.22	0.18	C	0.66	0.10	B	0.85	0.15	C	0.56	0.07	C
CATE	3	0.54	1.11	0.23	C	0.60	0.12	B	0.92	0.14	C	0.55	0.08	C
CATE	4	0.54	1.25	0.17	C	0.68	0.09	B	0.71	0.12	C	0.49	0.07	C
CATO	1	0.64	1.24	0.02	B	0.79	0.01	A	0.83	0.10	C	0.65	0.03	C
CATO	2	0.64	1.15	0.01	B	0.73	0.01	A	0.85	0.15	C	0.62	0.03	C
CATO	3	0.64	1.12	0.01	B	0.72	0.01	A	0.92	0.14	C	0.66	0.04	C
CATO	4	0.64	1.16	0.01	B	0.74	0.01	A	0.71	0.12	C	0.53	0.04	C
CADE	1	0.40	1.34	0.02	B	0.54	0.01	A	0.83	0.10	C	0.45	0.03	C
CADE	2	0.40	1.30	0.01	B	0.52	0.01	A	0.84	0.06	B	0.44	0.03	A
CADE	3	0.40	0.83	0.01	B	0.33	0.00	A	0.92	0.14	C	0.30	0.03	C
CADE	4	0.40	1.19	0.02	B	0.48	0.01	A	0.71	0.12	C	0.34	0.04	C
CAOZ	1	0.40	1.47	0.31	C	0.59	0.12	B	0.83	0.10	C	0.49	0.08	C
CAOZ	2	0.40	1.22	0.18	C	0.49	0.07	B	0.85	0.15	C	0.42	0.05	C
CAOZ	3	0.40	1.11	0.23	C	0.44	0.09	B	0.92	0.14	C	0.40	0.05	C
CAOZ	4	0.40	1.25	0.17	C	0.50	0.07	B	0.71	0.12	C	0.36	0.06	C
CAPU	1	0.40	1.47	0.31	C	0.59	0.12	B	0.83	0.10	C	0.49	0.08	C
CAPU	2	0.40	1.22	0.18	C	0.49	0.07	B	0.85	0.15	C	0.42	0.05	C
CAPU	3	0.40	1.11	0.23	C	0.44	0.09	B	0.92	0.14	C	0.40	0.05	C
CAPU	4	0.40	1.25	0.17	C	0.50	0.07	B	0.71	0.12	C	0.36	0.06	C
CASTA	1	0.42	1.47	0.31	C	0.62	0.13	B	0.83	0.10	C	0.51	0.09	C
CASTA	2	0.42	1.22	0.18	C	0.51	0.08	B	0.85	0.15	C	0.43	0.05	C
CASTA	3	0.42	1.11	0.23	C	0.47	0.10	B	0.92	0.14	C	0.43	0.06	C
CASTA	4	0.42	1.25	0.17	C	0.53	0.07	B	0.71	0.12	C	0.38	0.06	C
CATAL	1	0.38	1.47	0.31	C	0.56	0.12	B	0.83	0.10	C	0.46	0.07	C
CATAL	2	0.38	1.22	0.18	C	0.46	0.07	B	0.85	0.15	C	0.39	0.04	C
CATAL	3	0.38	1.11	0.23	C	0.42	0.09	B	0.92	0.14	C	0.39	0.05	C
CATAL	4	0.38	1.25	0.17	C	0.48	0.07	B	0.71	0.12	C	0.34	0.05	C
CELA	1	0.47	1.47	0.31	C	0.69	0.14	B	0.83	0.10	C	0.57	0.10	C

(Appendix 4 continued on next page)

(Appendix 4 continued)

Species code	Size class	Bole init density	Branch-bole ratio	Uncert B-B ratio	Uncert_bb ratio code	FWD initial density	Uncert FWD density	Uncert FWD code	Relative density	Uncert Rel density	Uncert Rel Den code	Decayed density	Uncert Decayed density	Uncert Decayed code
CELA	2	0.47	1.22	0.18	C	0.57	0.09	B	0.85	0.15	C	0.49	0.06	C
CELA	3	0.47	1.11	0.23	C	0.52	0.11	B	0.92	0.14	C	0.48	0.07	C
CELA	4	0.47	1.25	0.17	C	0.59	0.08	B	0.71	0.12	C	0.42	0.06	C
CEOC	1	0.49	1.47	0.31	C	0.72	0.15	B	0.83	0.10	C	0.60	0.11	C
CEOC	2	0.49	1.22	0.18	C	0.60	0.09	B	0.85	0.15	C	0.51	0.06	C
CEOC	3	0.49	1.11	0.23	C	0.54	0.11	B	0.92	0.14	C	0.50	0.07	C
CEOC	4	0.49	1.25	0.17	C	0.61	0.08	B	0.71	0.12	C	0.44	0.07	C
CESP	1	0.49	1.47	0.31	C	0.72	0.15	B	0.83	0.10	C	0.60	0.11	C
CESP	2	0.49	1.22	0.18	C	0.60	0.09	B	0.85	0.15	C	0.51	0.06	C
CESP	3	0.49	1.11	0.23	C	0.54	0.11	B	0.92	0.14	C	0.50	0.07	C
CESP	4	0.49	1.25	0.17	C	0.61	0.08	B	0.71	0.12	C	0.44	0.07	C
CECA	1	0.58	1.47	0.31	C	0.85	0.18	B	0.83	0.10	C	0.70	0.16	C
CECA	2	0.58	1.22	0.18	C	0.71	0.11	B	0.85	0.15	C	0.61	0.08	C
CECA	3	0.58	1.11	0.23	C	0.64	0.13	B	0.92	0.14	C	0.59	0.09	C
CECA	4	0.58	1.25	0.17	C	0.73	0.10	B	0.71	0.12	C	0.52	0.08	C
CEIN	1	1.00	1.47	0.31	C	1.47	0.31	B	0.83	0.10	C	1.22	0.46	C
CEIN	2	1.00	1.22	0.18	C	1.22	0.18	B	0.85	0.15	C	1.04	0.22	C
CEIN	3	1.00	1.11	0.23	C	1.11	0.23	B	0.92	0.14	C	1.02	0.26	C
CEIN	4	1.00	1.25	0.17	C	1.25	0.17	B	0.71	0.12	C	0.89	0.22	C
CELE	1	1.00	1.47	0.31	C	1.47	0.31	B	0.83	0.10	C	1.22	0.46	C
CELE	2	1.00	1.22	0.18	C	1.22	0.18	B	0.85	0.15	C	1.04	0.22	C
CELE	3	1.00	1.11	0.23	C	1.11	0.23	B	0.92	0.14	C	1.02	0.26	C
CELE	4	1.00	1.25	0.17	C	1.25	0.17	B	0.71	0.12	C	0.89	0.22	C
CEMO	1	1.00	1.47	0.31	C	1.47	0.31	B	0.83	0.10	C	1.22	0.46	C
CEMO	2	1.00	1.22	0.18	C	1.22	0.18	B	0.85	0.15	C	1.04	0.22	C
CEMO	3	1.00	1.11	0.23	C	1.11	0.23	B	0.92	0.14	C	1.02	0.26	C
CEMO	4	1.00	1.25	0.17	C	1.25	0.17	B	0.71	0.12	C	0.89	0.22	C
CHLA	1	0.39	1.47	0.31	C	0.57	0.12	B	0.82	0.19	C	0.47	0.08	C
CHLA	2	0.39	1.22	0.18	C	0.48	0.07	B	1.03	0.13	C	0.49	0.04	C
CHLA	3	0.39	1.11	0.23	C	0.43	0.09	B	0.95	0.12	C	0.41	0.05	C
CHLA	4	0.39	1.25	0.17	C	0.49	0.07	B	0.80	0.12	C	0.39	0.07	C
CHNO	1	0.42	1.47	0.31	C	0.62	0.13	B	0.82	0.19	C	0.51	0.09	C
CHNO	2	0.42	1.22	0.18	C	0.51	0.08	B	1.03	0.13	C	0.52	0.05	C
CHNO	3	0.42	1.11	0.23	C	0.47	0.10	B	0.95	0.12	C	0.45	0.06	C
CHNO	4	0.42	1.25	0.17	C	0.53	0.07	B	0.80	0.12	C	0.42	0.07	C
CHTH	1	0.31	1.47	0.31	C	0.46	0.09	B	0.82	0.19	C	0.38	0.06	C
CHTH	2	0.31	1.22	0.18	C	0.38	0.06	B	1.03	0.13	C	0.39	0.03	C
CHTH	3	0.31	1.11	0.23	C	0.34	0.07	B	0.95	0.12	C	0.32	0.04	C
CHTH	4	0.31	1.25	0.17	C	0.39	0.05	B	0.80	0.12	C	0.31	0.06	C
CLLU	1	0.52	1.47	0.31	C	0.76	0.16	B	0.83	0.10	C	0.63	0.13	C
CLLU	2	0.52	1.22	0.18	C	0.63	0.10	B	0.85	0.15	C	0.54	0.07	C

60

Species code	Size class	Bole init density	Branch-bole ratio	Uncert B-B ratio	Uncert_bb ratio code	FWD initial density	Uncert FWD density	Uncert FWD code	Relative density	Uncert Rel density	Uncert Rel Den code	Decayed density	Uncert Decayed density	Uncert Decayed code
CLLU	3	0.52	1.11	0.23	C	0.58	0.12	B	0.92	0.14	C	0.53	0.08	C
CLLU	4	0.52	1.25	0.17	C	0.65	0.09	B	0.71	0.12	C	0.46	0.07	C
COFL	1	0.64	1.47	0.31	C	0.94	0.20	B	0.83	0.10	C	0.78	0.19	C
COFL	2	0.64	1.22	0.18	C	0.78	0.12	B	0.85	0.15	C	0.66	0.10	C
COFL	3	0.64	1.11	0.23	C	0.71	0.15	B	0.92	0.14	C	0.65	0.11	C
COFL	4	0.64	1.25	0.17	C	0.80	0.11	B	0.71	0.12	C	0.57	0.10	C
CONU	1	0.58	1.47	0.31	C	0.85	0.18	B	0.83	0.10	C	0.70	0.16	C
CONU	2	0.58	1.22	0.18	C	0.71	0.11	B	0.85	0.15	C	0.61	0.08	C
CONU	3	0.58	1.11	0.23	C	0.64	0.13	B	0.92	0.14	C	0.59	0.09	C
CONU	4	0.58	1.25	0.17	C	0.73	0.10	B	0.71	0.12	C	0.52	0.08	C
COSP	1	0.64	1.47	0.31	C	0.94	0.20	B	0.83	0.10	C	0.78	0.19	C
COSP	2	0.64	1.22	0.18	C	0.78	0.12	B	0.85	0.15	C	0.66	0.10	C
COSP	3	0.64	1.11	0.23	C	0.71	0.15	B	0.92	0.14	C	0.65	0.11	C
COSP	4	0.64	1.25	0.17	C	0.80	0.11	B	0.71	0.12	C	0.57	0.10	C
COOB	1	0.47	1.47	0.31	C	0.69	0.14	B	0.83	0.10	C	0.57	0.10	C
COOB	2	0.47	1.22	0.18	C	0.57	0.09	B	0.85	0.15	C	0.49	0.06	C
COOB	3	0.47	1.11	0.23	C	0.52	0.11	B	0.92	0.14	C	0.48	0.07	C
COOB	4	0.47	1.25	0.17	C	0.59	0.08	B	0.71	0.12	C	0.42	0.06	C
CRSP	1	0.62	1.47	0.31	C	0.91	0.19	B	0.83	0.10	C	0.75	0.18	C
CRSP	2	0.62	1.22	0.18	C	0.76	0.11	B	0.85	0.15	C	0.65	0.09	C
CRSP	3	0.62	1.11	0.23	C	0.69	0.14	B	0.92	0.14	C	0.63	0.10	C
CRSP	4	0.62	1.25	0.17	C	0.78	0.11	B	0.71	0.12	C	0.56	0.10	C
CUSP	1	0.44	1.47	0.31	C	0.65	0.13	B	0.83	0.10	C	0.54	0.09	C
CUSP	2	0.44	1.22	0.18	C	0.54	0.08	B	0.85	0.15	C	0.46	0.05	C
CUSP	3	0.44	1.11	0.23	C	0.49	0.10	B	0.92	0.14	C	0.45	0.06	C
CUSP	4	0.44	1.25	0.17	C	0.55	0.08	B	0.71	0.12	C	0.39	0.06	C
DIVI	1	0.64	1.47	0.31	C	0.94	0.20	B	0.83	0.10	C	0.78	0.19	C
DIVI	2	0.64	1.22	0.18	C	0.78	0.12	B	0.85	0.15	C	0.66	0.10	C
DIVI	3	0.64	1.11	0.23	C	0.71	0.15	B	0.92	0.14	C	0.65	0.11	C
DIVI	4	0.64	1.25	0.17	C	0.80	0.11	B	0.71	0.12	C	0.57	0.10	C
EUSP	1	0.67	1.47	0.31	C	0.98	0.20	B	0.83	0.10	C	0.81	0.20	C
EUSP	2	0.67	1.22	0.18	C	0.82	0.12	B	0.85	0.15	C	0.70	0.10	C
EUSP	3	0.67	1.11	0.23	C	0.74	0.15	B	0.92	0.14	C	0.68	0.12	C
EUSP	4	0.67	1.25	0.17	C	0.84	0.12	B	0.71	0.12	C	0.60	0.11	C
FAGR	1	0.56	1.26	0.02	B	0.70	0.01	A	0.83	0.10	C	0.58	0.03	A
FAGR	2	0.56	1.06	0.02	B	0.60	0.01	A	0.77	0.04	B	0.46	0.03	A
FAGR	3	0.56	1.04	0.01	B	0.58	0.00	A	0.92	0.14	C	0.53	0.03	A
FAGR	4	0.56	1.11	0.02	B	0.62	0.01	A	0.66	0.04	B	0.41	0.03	A
FRAM	1	0.55	1.47	0.31	C	0.81	0.17	B	0.83	0.10	C	0.67	0.14	C
FRAM	2	0.55	1.22	0.18	C	0.67	0.10	B	0.85	0.15	C	0.57	0.07	C
FRAM	3	0.55	1.11	0.23	C	0.61	0.13	B	0.92	0.14	C	0.56	0.09	C

(Appendix 4 continued on next page)

(Appendix 4 continued)

Species code	Size class	Bole init density	Branch-bole ratio	Uncert B-B ratio	Uncert_bb ratio code	FWD initial density	Uncert FWD density	Uncert FWD code	Relative density	Uncert Rel density	Uncert Rel Den code	Decayed density	Uncert Decayed density	Uncert Decayed code
FRAM	4	0.55	1.25	0.17	C	0.69	0.10	B	0.71	0.12	C	0.49	0.08	C
FRLA	1	0.50	1.47	0.31	C	0.74	0.15	B	0.83	0.10	C	0.61	0.12	C
FRLA	2	0.50	1.22	0.18	C	0.61	0.09	B	0.85	0.15	C	0.52	0.06	C
FRLA	3	0.50	1.11	0.23	C	0.55	0.11	B	0.92	0.14	C	0.50	0.07	C
FRLA	4	0.50	1.25	0.17	C	0.63	0.09	B	0.71	0.12	C	0.45	0.07	C
FRNI	1	0.45	1.47	0.31	C	0.66	0.14	B	0.83	0.10	C	0.55	0.10	C
FRNI	2	0.45	1.22	0.18	C	0.55	0.08	B	0.85	0.15	C	0.47	0.05	C
FRNI	3	0.45	1.11	0.23	C	0.50	0.10	B	0.92	0.14	C	0.46	0.06	C
FRNI	4	0.45	1.25	0.17	C	0.56	0.08	B	0.71	0.12	C	0.40	0.06	C
FRPE	1	0.53	1.47	0.31	C	0.78	0.16	B	0.83	0.10	C	0.65	0.13	C
FRPE	2	0.53	1.22	0.18	C	0.65	0.10	B	0.85	0.15	C	0.55	0.07	C
FRPE	3	0.53	1.11	0.23	C	0.59	0.12	B	0.92	0.14	C	0.54	0.08	C
FRPE	4	0.53	1.25	0.17	C	0.66	0.09	B	0.71	0.12	C	0.47	0.07	C
FRPR	1	0.54	1.47	0.31	C	0.79	0.16	B	0.83	0.10	C	0.65	0.13	C
FRPR	2	0.54	1.22	0.18	C	0.66	0.10	B	0.85	0.15	C	0.56	0.07	C
FRPR	3	0.54	1.11	0.23	C	0.60	0.12	B	0.92	0.14	C	0.55	0.08	C
FRPR	4	0.54	1.25	0.17	C	0.68	0.09	B	0.71	0.12	C	0.49	0.07	C
FRQU	1	0.53	1.47	0.31	C	0.78	0.16	B	0.83	0.10	C	0.65	0.13	C
FRQU	2	0.53	1.22	0.18	C	0.65	0.10	B	0.85	0.15	C	0.55	0.07	C
FRQU	3	0.53	1.11	0.23	C	0.59	0.12	B	0.92	0.14	C	0.54	0.08	C
FRQU	4	0.53	1.25	0.17	C	0.66	0.09	B	0.71	0.12	C	0.47	0.07	C
FRSP	1	0.54	1.47	0.31	C	0.79	0.16	B	0.83	0.10	C	0.65	0.13	C
FRSP	2	0.54	1.22	0.18	C	0.66	0.10	B	0.85	0.15	C	0.56	0.07	C
FRSP	3	0.54	1.11	0.23	C	0.60	0.12	B	0.92	0.14	C	0.55	0.08	C
FRSP	4	0.54	1.25	0.17	C	0.68	0.09	B	0.71	0.12	C	0.49	0.07	C
GLAQ	1	0.60	1.47	0.31	C	0.88	0.18	B	0.83	0.10	C	0.73	0.16	C
GLAQ	2	0.60	1.22	0.18	C	0.73	0.11	B	0.85	0.15	C	0.62	0.09	C
GLAQ	3	0.60	1.11	0.23	C	0.66	0.14	B	0.92	0.14	C	0.61	0.10	C
GLAQ	4	0.60	1.25	0.17	C	0.75	0.10	B	0.71	0.12	C	0.54	0.09	C
GLTR	1	0.60	1.47	0.31	C	0.88	0.18	B	0.83	0.10	C	0.73	0.16	C
GLTR	2	0.60	1.22	0.18	C	0.73	0.11	B	0.85	0.15	C	0.62	0.09	C
GLTR	3	0.60	1.11	0.23	C	0.66	0.14	B	0.92	0.14	C	0.61	0.10	C
GLTR	4	0.60	1.25	0.17	C	0.75	0.10	B	0.71	0.12	C	0.54	0.09	C
GOLA	1	0.37	1.47	0.31	C	0.54	0.11	B	0.83	0.10	C	0.45	0.07	C
GOLA	2	0.37	1.22	0.18	C	0.45	0.07	B	0.85	0.15	C	0.38	0.04	C
GOLA	3	0.37	1.11	0.23	C	0.41	0.08	B	0.92	0.14	C	0.38	0.05	C
GOLA	4	0.37	1.25	0.17	C	0.46	0.06	B	0.71	0.12	C	0.33	0.05	C
GYDI	1	0.50	1.47	0.31	C	0.74	0.15	B	0.83	0.10	C	0.61	0.12	C
GYDI	2	0.50	1.22	0.18	C	0.61	0.09	B	0.85	0.15	C	0.52	0.06	C
GYDI	3	0.50	1.11	0.23	C	0.55	0.11	B	0.92	0.14	C	0.50	0.07	C
GYDI	4	0.50	1.25	0.17	C	0.63	0.09	B	0.71	0.12	C	0.45	0.07	C

Species code	Size class	Bole init density	Branch-bole ratio	Uncert B-B ratio	Uncert_bb ratio code	FWD initial density	Uncert FWD density	Uncert FWD code	Relative density	Uncert Rel density	Uncert Rel Den code	Decayed density	Uncert Decayed density	Uncert Decayed code
HASP	1	0.32	1.47	0.31	C	0.47	0.10	B	0.83	0.10	C	0.39	0.06	C
HASP	2	0.32	1.22	0.18	C	0.39	0.06	B	1.09	0.06	B	0.43	0.02	A
HASP	3	0.32	1.11	0.23	C	0.35	0.07	B	0.92	0.14	C	0.32	0.04	C
HASP	4	0.32	1.25	0.17	C	0.40	0.06	B	0.89	0.08	B	0.36	0.03	A
HARDW	1	0.51	1.28	0.07	B	0.65	0.03	A	0.83	0.10	C	0.54	0.04	C
HARDW	2	0.51	1.13	0.03	B	0.58	0.01	A	0.63	0.02	B	0.37	0.01	A
HARDW	3	0.51	1.11	0.23	C	0.56	0.12	B	0.92	0.14	C	0.51	0.08	C
HARDW	4	0.51	1.25	0.17	C	0.64	0.09	B	0.54	0.03	B	0.35	0.02	A
ILOP	1	0.50	1.47	0.31	C	0.74	0.15	B	0.83	0.10	C	0.61	0.12	C
ILOP	2	0.50	1.22	0.18	C	0.61	0.09	B	0.85	0.15	C	0.52	0.06	C
ILOP	3	0.50	1.11	0.23	C	0.55	0.11	B	0.92	0.14	C	0.50	0.07	C
ILOP	4	0.50	1.25	0.17	C	0.63	0.09	B	0.71	0.12	C	0.45	0.07	C
JUCI	1	0.36	1.47	0.31	C	0.53	0.11	B	0.83	0.10	C	0.44	0.07	C
JUCI	2	0.36	1.22	0.18	C	0.44	0.07	B	0.85	0.15	C	0.38	0.04	C
JUCI	3	0.36	1.11	0.23	C	0.40	0.08	B	0.92	0.14	C	0.37	0.05	C
JUCI	4	0.36	1.25	0.17	C	0.45	0.06	B	0.71	0.12	C	0.32	0.05	C
JUSP	1	0.51	1.47	0.31	C	0.75	0.16	B	0.83	0.10	C	0.62	0.12	C
JUSP	2	0.51	1.22	0.18	C	0.62	0.09	B	0.85	0.15	C	0.53	0.06	C
JUSP	3	0.51	1.11	0.23	C	0.56	0.12	B	0.95	0.12	C	0.53	0.07	C
JUSP	4	0.51	1.25	0.17	C	0.64	0.09	B	0.80	0.12	C	0.51	0.08	C
JUNI	1	0.51	1.47	0.31	C	0.75	0.16	B	0.83	0.10	C	0.62	0.12	C
JUNI	2	0.51	1.22	0.18	C	0.62	0.09	B	0.85	0.15	C	0.53	0.06	C
JUNI	3	0.51	1.11	0.23	C	0.56	0.12	B	0.92	0.14	C	0.51	0.08	C
JUNI	4	0.51	1.25	0.17	C	0.64	0.09	B	0.71	0.12	C	0.46	0.07	C
JUMO	1	0.45	1.47	0.31	C	0.66	0.14	B	0.82	0.19	C	0.54	0.10	C
JUMO	2	0.45	1.22	0.18	C	0.55	0.08	B	1.03	0.13	C	0.56	0.05	C
JUMO	3	0.45	1.11	0.23	C	0.50	0.10	B	0.95	0.12	C	0.48	0.06	C
JUMO	4	0.45	1.25	0.17	C	0.56	0.08	B	0.80	0.12	C	0.45	0.07	C
JUOC	1	0.44	1.47	0.31	C	0.65	0.13	B	0.82	0.19	C	0.54	0.10	C
JUOC	2	0.44	1.22	0.18	C	0.54	0.08	B	1.03	0.13	C	0.55	0.05	C
JUOC	3	0.44	1.11	0.23	C	0.49	0.10	B	0.95	0.12	C	0.47	0.06	C
JUOC	4	0.44	1.25	0.17	C	0.55	0.08	B	0.80	0.12	C	0.44	0.07	C
JUSP2	1	0.44	1.47	0.31	C	0.65	0.13	B	0.83	0.10	C	0.54	0.09	C
JUSP2	2	0.44	1.22	0.18	C	0.54	0.08	B	0.85	0.15	C	0.46	0.05	C
JUSP2	3	0.44	1.11	0.23	C	0.49	0.10	B	0.95	0.12	C	0.47	0.06	C
JUSP2	4	0.44	1.25	0.17	C	0.55	0.08	B	0.80	0.12	C	0.44	0.07	C
JUVI	1	0.37	1.94	0.07	B	0.72	0.03	A	0.82	0.19	C	0.59	0.05	C
JUVI	2	0.37	1.38	0.03	B	0.51	0.01	A	1.03	0.13	C	0.52	0.03	C
JUVI	3	0.37	1.24	0.02	B	0.46	0.01	A	0.95	0.12	C	0.44	0.03	C
JUVI	4	0.37	1.48	0.05	B	0.55	0.02	A	0.80	0.12	C	0.44	0.06	C
LALA	1	0.49	1.47	0.31	C	0.72	0.15	B	0.69	0.01	A	0.50	0.05	B

(Appendix 4 continued on next page)

Species code	Size class	Bole init density	Branch-bole ratio	Uncert B-B ratio	Uncert_bb ratio code	FWD initial density	Uncert FWD density	Uncert FWD code	Relative density	Uncert Rel density	Uncert Rel Den code	Decayed density	Uncert Decayed density	Uncert Decayed code
LALA	2	0.49	1.22	0.18	C	0.60	0.09	B	0.86	0.01	A	0.52	0.05	B
LALA	3	0.49	1.11	0.23	C	0.54	0.11	B	1.01	0.01	A	0.55	0.05	B
LALA	4	0.49	1.25	0.17	C	0.61	0.08	B	0.71	0.12	C	0.44	0.07	C
LALY	1	0.48	1.47	0.31	C	0.71	0.15	B	0.83	0.10	C	0.59	0.11	C
LALY	2	0.48	1.22	0.18	C	0.58	0.09	B	0.85	0.15	C	0.49	0.06	C
LALY	3	0.48	1.11	0.23	C	0.53	0.11	B	0.92	0.14	C	0.49	0.07	C
LALY	4	0.48	1.25	0.17	C	0.60	0.08	B	0.71	0.12	C	0.43	0.06	B
LAOC	1	0.48	1.47	0.31	C	0.71	0.15	B	0.70	0.06	A	0.50	0.05	B
LAOC	2	0.48	1.22	0.18	C	0.58	0.09	B	0.93	0.09	B	0.54	0.05	C
LAOC	3	0.48	1.11	0.23	C	0.53	0.11	B	0.92	0.14	C	0.49	0.07	C
LAOC	4	0.48	1.25	0.17	C	0.60	0.08	B	0.92	0.09	B	0.55	0.05	B
LASP	1	0.44	1.47	0.31	C	0.65	0.13	B	0.83	0.10	C	0.54	0.09	C
LASP	2	0.44	1.22	0.18	C	0.54	0.08	B	0.85	0.15	C	0.46	0.05	C
LASP	3	0.44	1.11	0.23	C	0.49	0.10	B	0.92	0.14	C	0.45	0.06	C
LASP	4	0.44	1.25	0.17	C	0.55	0.08	B	0.71	0.12	C	0.39	0.06	C
LIST	1	0.46	1.30	0.02	B	0.60	0.01	A	0.83	0.10	C	0.50	0.03	A
LIST	2	0.46	1.16	0.03	B	0.53	0.01	A	0.85	0.15	C	0.45	0.03	C
LIST	3	0.46	1.12	0.02	B	0.52	0.01	A	0.92	0.14	C	0.48	0.04	A
LIST	4	0.46	1.18	0.05	B	0.54	0.02	A	0.71	0.12	C	0.39	0.04	A
LITU	1	0.40	1.38	0.02	B	0.55	0.01	A	0.83	0.10	C	0.46	0.03	C
LITU	2	0.40	1.11	0.02	B	0.44	0.01	A	0.93	0.03	B	0.41	0.01	C
LITU	3	0.40	1.11	0.02	B	0.44	0.01	A	0.92	0.14	C	0.40	0.04	C
LITU	4	0.40	1.18	0.02	B	0.47	0.01	A	0.71	0.05	B	0.33	0.03	C
LIDE	1	0.58	1.47	0.31	C	0.85	0.18	B	0.83	0.10	C	0.70	0.16	C
LIDE	2	0.58	1.22	0.18	C	0.71	0.11	B	0.85	0.15	C	0.61	0.08	C
LIDE	3	0.58	1.11	0.23	C	0.64	0.13	B	0.92	0.14	C	0.59	0.09	C
LIDE	4	0.58	1.25	0.17	C	0.73	0.10	B	0.71	0.12	C	0.52	0.08	C
MAPO	1	0.76	1.47	0.31	C	1.12	0.23	B	0.83	0.10	C	0.93	0.26	C
MAPO	2	0.76	1.22	0.18	C	0.93	0.14	B	0.85	0.15	C	0.79	0.13	C
MAPO	3	0.76	1.11	0.23	C	0.84	0.17	B	0.92	0.14	C	0.77	0.15	C
MAPO	4	0.76	1.25	0.17	C	0.95	0.13	B	0.71	0.12	C	0.68	0.13	C
MASP	1	0.45	1.47	0.31	C	0.66	0.14	B	0.83	0.10	C	0.55	0.10	C
MASP	2	0.45	1.22	0.18	C	0.55	0.08	B	0.85	0.15	C	0.47	0.05	C
MASP	3	0.45	1.11	0.23	C	0.50	0.10	B	0.92	0.14	C	0.46	0.06	C
MASP	4	0.45	1.25	0.17	C	0.56	0.08	B	0.71	0.12	C	0.40	0.06	C
MASP2	1	0.61	1.47	0.31	C	0.90	0.19	B	0.83	0.10	C	0.75	0.17	C
MASP2	2	0.61	1.22	0.18	C	0.74	0.11	B	0.85	0.15	C	0.63	0.09	C
MASP2	3	0.61	1.11	0.23	C	0.68	0.14	B	0.92	0.14	C	0.62	0.10	C
MASP2	4	0.61	1.25	0.17	C	0.76	0.11	B	0.71	0.12	C	0.54	0.09	C
MEAZ	1	0.47	1.47	0.31	C	0.69	0.14	B	0.83	0.10	C	0.57	0.10	C
MEAZ	2	0.47	1.22	0.18	C	0.57	0.09	B	0.85	0.15	C	0.49	0.06	C

Species code	Size class	Bole init density	Branch-bole ratio	Uncert B-B ratio	Uncert_bb ratio code	FWD initial density	Uncert FWD density	Uncert FWD code	Relative density	Uncert Rel density	Uncert Rel Den code	Decayed density	Uncert Decayed density	Uncert Decayed code
MEAZ	3	0.47	1.11	0.23	C	0.52	0.11	B	0.92	0.14	C	0.48	0.07	C
MEAZ	4	0.47	1.25	0.17	C	0.59	0.08	B	0.71	0.12	C	0.42	0.06	C
MOAL	1	0.59	1.47	0.31	C	0.87	0.18	B	0.83	0.10	C	0.72	0.16	C
MOAL	2	0.59	1.22	0.18	C	0.72	0.11	B	0.85	0.15	C	0.61	0.09	C
MOAL	3	0.59	1.11	0.23	C	0.65	0.13	B	0.92	0.14	C	0.60	0.09	C
MOAL	4	0.59	1.25	0.17	C	0.74	0.10	B	0.71	0.12	C	0.53	0.09	C
MORU	1	0.59	1.47	0.31	C	0.87	0.18	B	0.83	0.10	C	0.72	0.16	C
MORU	2	0.59	1.22	0.18	C	0.72	0.11	B	0.85	0.15	C	0.61	0.09	C
MORU	3	0.59	1.11	0.23	C	0.65	0.13	B	0.92	0.14	C	0.60	0.09	C
MORU	4	0.59	1.25	0.17	C	0.74	0.10	B	0.71	0.12	C	0.53	0.09	C
MOSP	1	0.59	1.47	0.31	C	0.87	0.18	B	0.83	0.10	C	0.72	0.16	C
MOSP	2	0.59	1.22	0.18	C	0.72	0.11	B	0.85	0.15	C	0.61	0.09	C
MOSP	3	0.59	1.11	0.23	C	0.65	0.13	B	0.92	0.14	C	0.60	0.09	C
MOSP	4	0.59	1.25	0.17	C	0.74	0.10	B	0.71	0.12	C	0.53	0.09	C
NYAQ	1	0.46	1.47	0.31	C	0.68	0.14	B	0.83	0.10	C	0.56	0.10	C
NYAQ	2	0.46	1.22	0.18	C	0.56	0.08	B	0.85	0.15	C	0.48	0.05	C
NYAQ	3	0.46	1.11	0.23	C	0.51	0.10	B	0.92	0.14	C	0.47	0.06	C
NYAQ	4	0.46	1.25	0.17	C	0.58	0.08	B	0.71	0.12	C	0.41	0.06	C
NYOG	1	0.46	1.47	0.31	C	0.68	0.14	B	0.83	0.10	C	0.56	0.10	C
NYOG	2	0.46	1.22	0.18	C	0.56	0.08	B	0.85	0.15	C	0.48	0.05	C
NYOG	3	0.46	1.11	0.23	C	0.51	0.10	B	0.92	0.14	C	0.47	0.06	C
NYOG	4	0.46	1.25	0.17	C	0.58	0.08	B	0.71	0.12	C	0.41	0.06	C
NYSY	1	0.46	1.47	0.31	C	0.68	0.14	B	0.83	0.10	C	0.56	0.10	C
NYSY	2	0.46	1.22	0.18	C	0.56	0.08	B	0.85	0.15	C	0.48	0.05	C
NYSY	3	0.46	1.11	0.23	C	0.51	0.10	B	0.92	0.14	C	0.47	0.06	C
NYSY	4	0.46	1.25	0.17	C	0.58	0.08	B	0.71	0.12	C	0.41	0.06	C
OLTE	1	1.00	1.47	0.31	C	1.47	0.31	B	0.83	0.10	C	1.22	0.46	C
OLTE	2	1.00	1.22	0.18	C	1.22	0.18	B	0.85	0.15	C	1.04	0.22	C
OLTE	3	1.00	1.11	0.23	C	1.11	0.23	B	0.92	0.14	C	1.02	0.26	C
OLTE	4	1.00	1.25	0.17	C	1.25	0.17	B	0.71	0.12	C	0.89	0.22	C
OSVI	1	0.63	1.47	0.31	C	0.93	0.19	B	0.83	0.10	C	0.77	0.18	C
OSVI	2	0.63	1.22	0.18	C	0.77	0.12	B	0.85	0.15	C	0.66	0.10	C
OSVI	3	0.63	1.11	0.23	C	0.70	0.14	B	0.92	0.14	C	0.64	0.10	C
OSVI	4	0.63	1.25	0.17	C	0.79	0.11	B	0.71	0.12	C	0.56	0.10	C
OXAR	1	0.50	1.47	0.31	C	0.74	0.15	B	0.83	0.10	C	0.61	0.12	C
OXAR	2	0.50	1.22	0.18	C	0.61	0.09	B	0.85	0.15	C	0.52	0.06	C
OXAR	3	0.50	1.11	0.23	C	0.55	0.11	B	0.92	0.14	C	0.50	0.07	C
OXAR	4	0.50	1.25	0.17	C	0.63	0.09	B	0.71	0.12	C	0.45	0.07	C
PATO	1	0.38	1.47	0.31	C	0.56	0.12	B	0.83	0.10	C	0.46	0.07	C
PATO	2	0.38	1.22	0.18	C	0.46	0.07	B	0.85	0.15	C	0.39	0.04	C
PATO	3	0.38	1.11	0.23	C	0.42	0.09	B	0.92	0.14	C	0.39	0.05	C

(Appendix 4 continued on next page)

(Appendix 4 continued)

Species code	Size class	Bole init density	Branch-bole ratio	Uncert B-B ratio	Uncert_bb ratio code	FWD initial density	Uncert FWD density	Uncert FWD code	Relative density	Uncert Rel density	Uncert Rel Den code	Decayed density	Uncert Decayed density	Uncert Decayed code
PATO	4	0.38	1.25	0.17	C	0.48	0.07	B	0.71	0.12	C	0.34	0.05	C
PEBO	1	0.51	1.47	0.31	C	0.75	0.16	B	0.83	0.10	C	0.62	0.12	C
PEBO	2	0.51	1.22	0.18	C	0.62	0.09	B	0.85	0.15	C	0.53	0.06	C
PEBO	3	0.51	1.11	0.23	C	0.56	0.12	B	0.92	0.14	C	0.51	0.08	C
PEBO	4	0.51	1.25	0.17	C	0.64	0.09	B	0.71	0.12	C	0.46	0.07	C
PIAB	1	0.38	1.47	0.31	C	0.56	0.12	B	0.82	0.19	C	0.46	0.08	C
PIAB	2	0.38	1.22	0.18	C	0.46	0.07	B	1.03	0.13	C	0.47	0.04	C
PIAB	3	0.38	1.11	0.23	C	0.42	0.09	B	0.95	0.12	C	0.40	0.05	C
PIAB	4	0.38	1.25	0.17	C	0.48	0.07	B	0.80	0.12	C	0.38	0.07	C
PIBR	1	0.33	1.47	0.31	C	0.49	0.10	B	0.82	0.19	C	0.40	0.07	C
PIBR	2	0.33	1.22	0.18	C	0.40	0.06	B	1.03	0.13	C	0.41	0.04	C
PIBR	3	0.33	1.11	0.23	C	0.37	0.08	B	0.95	0.12	C	0.35	0.04	C
PIBR	4	0.33	1.25	0.17	C	0.41	0.06	B	0.80	0.12	C	0.33	0.06	C
PIEN	1	0.33	2.09	0.07	B	0.69	0.02	A	0.49	0.05	B	0.34	0.03	B
PIEN	2	0.33	1.31	0.02	B	0.43	0.01	A	1.03	0.13	C	0.44	0.03	C
PIEN	3	0.33	1.38	0.03	B	0.45	0.01	A	0.95	0.12	C	0.43	0.03	C
PIEN	4	0.33	1.52	0.05	B	0.50	0.02	A	0.68	0.06	B	0.34	0.03	B
PIGL	1	0.37	1.47	0.31	C	0.54	0.11	B	0.92	0.02	A	0.50	0.05	B
PIGL	2	0.37	1.22	0.18	C	0.45	0.07	B	1.20	0.01	A	0.54	0.05	B
PIGL	3	0.37	1.11	0.23	C	0.41	0.08	B	1.07	0.01	A	0.44	0.04	B
PIGL	4	0.37	1.25	0.17	C	0.46	0.06	B	0.80	0.12	C	0.37	0.06	C
PIMA	1	0.38	1.47	0.31	C	0.56	0.12	B	0.92	0.02	A	0.51	0.05	B
PIMA	2	0.38	1.22	0.18	C	0.46	0.07	B	1.20	0.01	A	0.55	0.05	B
PIMA	3	0.38	1.11	0.23	C	0.42	0.09	B	1.17	0.01	A	0.49	0.05	B
PIMA	4	0.38	1.25	0.17	C	0.48	0.07	B	0.80	0.12	C	0.38	0.07	C
PIPU	1	0.38	1.47	0.31	C	0.56	0.12	B	0.82	0.19	C	0.46	0.08	C
PIPU	2	0.38	1.22	0.18	C	0.46	0.07	B	1.03	0.13	C	0.47	0.04	C
PIPU	3	0.38	1.11	0.23	C	0.42	0.09	B	0.95	0.12	C	0.40	0.05	C
PIPU	4	0.38	1.25	0.17	C	0.48	0.07	B	0.80	0.12	C	0.38	0.07	C
PIRU	1	0.38	1.47	0.31	C	0.56	0.12	B	0.82	0.19	C	0.46	0.08	C
PIRU	2	0.38	1.22	0.18	C	0.46	0.07	B	1.03	0.13	C	0.47	0.04	C
PIRU	3	0.38	1.11	0.23	C	0.42	0.09	B	0.95	0.12	C	0.40	0.05	C
PIRU	4	0.38	1.25	0.17	C	0.48	0.07	B	0.80	0.12	C	0.38	0.07	C
PISI	1	0.37	1.70	0.04	B	0.63	0.01	A	0.82	0.19	C	0.52	0.04	C
PISI	2	0.37	1.59	0.02	B	0.59	0.01	A	1.03	0.13	C	0.61	0.03	C
PISI	3	0.37	1.64	0.02	B	0.61	0.01	A	0.95	0.12	C	0.58	0.03	C
PISI	4	0.37	1.63	0.01	B	0.60	0.01	A	0.80	0.12	C	0.48	0.06	C
PICEA	1	0.38	1.47	0.31	C	0.56	0.12	B	0.82	0.19	C	0.46	0.08	C
PICEA	2	0.38	1.22	0.18	C	0.46	0.07	B	1.03	0.13	C	0.47	0.04	C
PICEA	3	0.38	1.11	0.23	C	0.42	0.09	B	0.95	0.12	C	0.40	0.05	C
PICEA	4	0.38	1.25	0.17	C	0.48	0.07	B	0.80	0.12	C	0.38	0.07	C

Species code	Size class	Bole init density	Branch-bole ratio	Uncert B-B ratio	Uncert_bb ratio code	FWD initial density	Uncert FWD density	Uncert FWD code	Relative density	Uncert Rel density	Uncert Rel Den code	Decayed density	Uncert Decayed density	Uncert Decayed code
PISP	4	0.39	1.32	0.17	C	0.52	0.07	B	0.80	0.12	C	0.41	0.07	C
PIAL	1	0.37	1.47	0.31	C	0.54	0.11	B	0.82	0.19	C	0.44	0.07	C
PIAL	2	0.37	1.22	0.18	C	0.45	0.07	B	1.03	0.13	C	0.46	0.04	C
PIAL	3	0.37	1.11	0.23	C	0.41	0.08	B	0.95	0.12	C	0.39	0.05	C
PIAL	4	0.37	1.25	0.17	C	0.46	0.06	B	0.80	0.12	C	0.37	0.06	C
PIAR	1	0.37	1.47	0.31	C	0.54	0.11	B	0.82	0.19	C	0.44	0.07	C
PIAR	2	0.37	1.22	0.18	C	0.45	0.07	B	1.03	0.13	C	0.46	0.04	C
PIAR	3	0.37	1.11	0.23	C	0.41	0.08	B	0.95	0.12	C	0.39	0.05	C
PIAR	4	0.37	1.25	0.17	C	0.46	0.06	B	0.80	0.12	C	0.37	0.06	C
PIAR2	1	0.37	1.47	0.31	C	0.54	0.11	B	0.82	0.19	C	0.44	0.07	C
PIAR2	2	0.37	1.22	0.18	C	0.45	0.07	B	1.03	0.13	C	0.46	0.04	C
PIAR2	3	0.37	1.11	0.23	C	0.41	0.08	B	0.95	0.12	C	0.39	0.05	C
PIAR2	4	0.37	1.25	0.17	C	0.46	0.06	B	0.80	0.12	C	0.37	0.06	C
PIAT	1	0.37	1.47	0.31	C	0.54	0.11	B	0.82	0.19	C	0.44	0.07	C
PIAT	2	0.37	1.22	0.18	C	0.45	0.07	B	1.03	0.13	C	0.46	0.04	C
PIAT	3	0.37	1.11	0.23	C	0.41	0.08	B	0.95	0.12	C	0.39	0.05	C
PIAT	4	0.37	1.25	0.17	C	0.46	0.07	B	0.80	0.12	C	0.37	0.06	C
PIBA	1	0.37	1.50	0.07	B	0.55	0.03	A	0.82	0.13	C	0.45	0.05	C
PIBA	2	0.37	1.29	0.18	A	0.48	0.03	A	1.03	0.12	C	0.49	0.03	C
PIBA	3	0.37	1.11	0.23	C	0.41	0.08	B	0.95	0.12	C	0.39	0.05	C
PIBA	4	0.37	1.25	0.17	C	0.46	0.06	B	0.80	0.12	C	0.37	0.06	C
PIBA2	1	0.40	1.47	0.31	C	0.59	0.12	B	0.78	0.02	A	0.46	0.04	B
PIBA2	2	0.40	1.22	0.18	C	0.49	0.07	B	0.98	0.01	A	0.48	0.04	B
PIBA2	3	0.40	1.11	0.23	C	0.44	0.09	B	1.00	0.01	A	0.44	0.04	B
PIBA2	4	0.40	1.25	0.17	C	0.50	0.07	B	0.80	0.12	C	0.40	0.07	B
PICL	1	0.46	1.47	0.31	C	0.68	0.14	B	0.82	0.19	C	0.56	0.10	C
PICL	2	0.46	1.22	0.18	C	0.56	0.08	B	1.03	0.13	C	0.57	0.05	C
PICL	3	0.46	1.11	0.23	C	0.51	0.10	B	0.95	0.12	C	0.49	0.06	C
PICL	4	0.46	1.25	0.17	C	0.58	0.08	B	0.80	0.12	C	0.46	0.07	C
PICO	1	0.38	1.60	0.02	B	0.61	0.01	A	0.82	0.04	A	0.50	0.05	B
PICO	2	0.38	1.23	0.01	B	0.47	0.01	A	1.07	0.03	A	0.51	0.05	B
PICO	3	0.38	1.13	0.01	B	0.43	0.00	A	1.02	0.10	B	0.44	0.04	B
PICO	4	0.38	1.30	0.01	B	0.49	0.01	A	0.84	0.08	B	0.41	0.04	B
PICO3	1	0.37	1.47	0.31	C	0.54	0.11	B	0.82	0.19	C	0.44	0.07	C
PICO3	2	0.37	1.22	0.18	C	0.45	0.07	B	1.03	0.13	C	0.46	0.04	C
PICO3	3	0.37	1.11	0.23	C	0.41	0.08	B	0.95	0.12	C	0.39	0.05	C
PICO3	4	0.37	1.25	0.17	C	0.46	0.06	B	0.80	0.12	C	0.37	0.06	C
PIDI	1	0.50	1.47	0.31	C	0.74	0.15	B	0.82	0.19	C	0.61	0.12	C
PIDI	2	0.50	1.22	0.18	C	0.61	0.09	B	1.03	0.13	C	0.63	0.06	C
PIDI	3	0.50	1.11	0.23	C	0.55	0.11	B	0.95	0.12	C	0.52	0.07	C
PIDI	4	0.50	1.25	0.17	C	0.63	0.09	B	0.80	0.12	C	0.50	0.08	C

(Appendix 4 continued on next page)

Species code	Size class	Bole init density	Branch-bole ratio	Uncert B-B ratio	Uncert_bb ratio code	FWD initial density	Uncert FWD density	Uncert FWD code	Relative density	Uncert Rel density	Uncert Rel Den code	Decayed density	Uncert Decayed density	Uncert Decayed code
PIEC	1	0.47	1.36	0.05	B	0.64	0.02	A	0.82	0.19	C	0.53	0.05	C
PIEC	2	0.47	1.11	0.03	B	0.52	0.01	A	1.03	0.13	C	0.53	0.03	C
PIEC	3	0.47	0.92	0.02	B	0.43	0.01	A	0.95	0.12	C	0.41	0.03	C
PIEC	4	0.47	1.12	0.03	B	0.53	0.01	A	0.80	0.12	C	0.42	0.06	C
PIED	1	0.50	1.47	0.31	C	0.74	0.15	B	0.82	0.19	C	0.61	0.12	C
PIED	2	0.50	1.22	0.18	C	0.61	0.09	B	1.03	0.13	C	0.63	0.06	C
PIED	3	0.50	1.11	0.23	C	0.55	0.11	B	0.95	0.12	C	0.52	0.07	C
PIED	4	0.50	1.25	0.17	C	0.63	0.09	B	0.80	0.12	C	0.50	0.08	C
PIEL	1	0.54	1.47	0.31	C	0.79	0.16	B	0.82	0.19	C	0.65	0.13	C
PIEL	2	0.54	1.22	0.18	C	0.66	0.10	B	1.03	0.13	C	0.68	0.07	C
PIEL	3	0.54	1.11	0.23	C	0.60	0.12	B	0.95	0.12	C	0.57	0.08	C
PIEL	4	0.54	1.25	0.17	C	0.68	0.09	B	0.80	0.12	C	0.54	0.08	C
PIEN2	1	0.37	1.86	0.06	B	0.69	0.02	A	0.82	0.19	C	0.57	0.05	C
PIEN2	2	0.37	1.17	0.02	B	0.43	0.01	A	1.03	0.13	C	0.44	0.03	C
PIEN2	3	0.37	1.23	0.02	B	0.45	0.01	A	0.95	0.12	C	0.43	0.03	C
PIEN2	4	0.37	1.36	0.05	B	0.50	0.02	A	0.80	0.12	C	0.40	0.06	C
PIFL	1	0.37	1.37	0.02	B	0.51	0.01	A	0.82	0.19	C	0.42	0.04	C
PIFL	2	0.37	1.17	0.02	B	0.43	0.01	A	1.03	0.13	C	0.44	0.03	C
PIFL	3	0.37	1.15	0.01	B	0.43	0.01	A	0.95	0.12	C	0.41	0.03	C
PIFL	4	0.37	1.21	0.02	B	0.45	0.01	A	0.80	0.12	C	0.36	0.06	C
PIGL2	1	0.41	1.47	0.31	C	0.60	0.13	B	0.82	0.19	C	0.49	0.09	C
PIGL2	2	0.41	1.22	0.18	C	0.50	0.08	B	1.03	0.13	C	0.51	0.05	C
PIGL2	3	0.41	1.11	0.23	C	0.45	0.09	B	0.95	0.12	C	0.43	0.05	C
PIGL2	4	0.41	1.25	0.17	C	0.51	0.07	B	0.80	0.12	C	0.41	0.07	C
PIJE	1	0.37	1.47	0.31	C	0.54	0.11	B	0.82	0.19	C	0.44	0.07	C
PIJE	2	0.37	1.22	0.18	C	0.45	0.07	B	1.03	0.13	C	0.46	0.04	C
PIJE	3	0.37	1.11	0.23	C	0.41	0.08	B	0.95	0.12	C	0.39	0.05	C
PIJE	4	0.37	1.25	0.17	C	0.46	0.06	B	0.80	0.12	C	0.37	0.06	C
PILA	1	0.34	1.47	0.31	C	0.50	0.10	B	0.82	0.19	C	0.41	0.07	C
PILA	2	0.34	1.22	0.18	C	0.41	0.06	B	1.03	0.13	C	0.42	0.04	C
PILA	3	0.34	1.11	0.23	C	0.38	0.08	B	0.95	0.12	C	0.36	0.04	C
PILA	4	0.34	1.25	0.17	C	0.43	0.06	B	0.80	0.12	C	0.34	0.06	C
PILE	1	0.37	1.47	0.31	C	0.54	0.11	B	0.82	0.19	C	0.44	0.07	C
PILE	2	0.37	1.22	0.18	C	0.45	0.07	B	1.03	0.13	C	0.46	0.04	C
PILE	3	0.37	1.11	0.23	C	0.41	0.08	B	0.95	0.12	C	0.39	0.05	C
PILE	4	0.37	1.25	0.17	C	0.46	0.06	B	0.80	0.12	C	0.37	0.06	C
PIMOP	1	0.50	1.47	0.31	C	0.74	0.15	B	0.82	0.19	C	0.61	0.12	C
PIMOP	2	0.50	1.22	0.18	C	0.61	0.09	B	1.03	0.13	C	0.63	0.06	C
PIMOP	3	0.50	1.11	0.23	C	0.55	0.11	B	0.95	0.12	C	0.52	0.07	C
PIMOP	4	0.50	1.25	0.17	C	0.63	0.09	B	0.80	0.12	C	0.50	0.08	C
PIMO	1	0.35	1.47	0.31	C	0.51	0.11	B	0.82	0.19	C	0.42	0.07	C

Species code	Size class	Bole init density	Branch-bole ratio	Uncert B-B ratio	Uncert_bb ratio code	FWD initial density	Uncert FWD density	Uncert FWD code	Relative density	Uncert Rel density	Uncert Rel Den code	Decayed density	Uncert Decayed density	Uncert Decayed code
PIMO	2	0.35	1.22	0.18	C	0.43	0.06	B	1.03	0.13	C	0.44	0.04	C
PIMO	3	0.35	1.11	0.23	C	0.39	0.08	B	0.95	0.12	C	0.37	0.04	C
PIMO	4	0.35	1.25	0.17	C	0.44	0.06	B	0.80	0.12	C	0.35	0.06	C
PIMU	1	0.37	1.47	0.31	C	0.54	0.11	B	0.82	0.19	C	0.44	0.07	C
PIMU	2	0.37	1.22	0.18	C	0.45	0.07	B	1.03	0.13	C	0.46	0.04	C
PIMU	3	0.37	1.11	0.23	C	0.41	0.08	B	0.95	0.12	C	0.39	0.05	C
PIMU	4	0.37	1.25	0.17	C	0.46	0.06	B	0.80	0.12	C	0.37	0.06	C
PINI	1	0.41	1.47	0.31	C	0.60	0.13	B	0.82	0.19	C	0.49	0.09	C
PINI	2	0.41	1.22	0.18	C	0.50	0.08	B	1.03	0.13	C	0.51	0.05	C
PINI	3	0.41	1.11	0.23	C	0.45	0.09	B	0.95	0.12	C	0.43	0.05	C
PINI	4	0.41	1.25	0.17	C	0.51	0.07	B	0.80	0.12	C	0.41	0.07	C
PIPA	1	0.54	1.47	0.31	C	0.79	0.16	B	0.82	0.19	C	0.65	0.13	C
PIPA	2	0.54	1.22	0.18	C	0.66	0.10	B	1.03	0.13	C	0.68	0.07	C
PIPA	3	0.54	1.11	0.23	C	0.60	0.12	B	0.95	0.12	C	0.57	0.08	C
PIPA	4	0.54	1.25	0.17	C	0.68	0.09	B	0.80	0.12	C	0.54	0.08	C
PIPO	1	0.38	1.44	0.02	B	0.55	0.01	A	0.89	0.11	A	0.49	0.05	C
PIPO	2	0.38	1.26	0.02	A	0.48	0.01	A	0.95	0.03	A	0.46	0.03	C
PIPO	3	0.38	1.08	0.03	A	0.41	0.01	A	0.82	0.01	A	0.34	0.02	C
PIPO	4	0.38	1.28	0.01	B	0.49	0.00	A	1.04	0.10	B	0.51	0.05	B
PIPU2	1	0.49	1.47	0.31	C	0.72	0.15	B	0.82	0.19	C	0.59	0.12	C
PIPU2	2	0.49	1.22	0.18	C	0.60	0.09	B	1.03	0.13	C	0.62	0.06	C
PIPU2	3	0.49	1.11	0.23	C	0.54	0.11	B	0.95	0.12	C	0.51	0.07	C
PIPU2	4	0.49	1.25	0.17	C	0.61	0.08	B	0.80	0.12	C	0.49	0.08	C
PIRA	1	0.37	1.47	0.31	C	0.54	0.11	B	0.82	0.19	C	0.44	0.07	C
PIRA	2	0.37	1.22	0.18	C	0.45	0.07	B	1.03	0.13	C	0.46	0.04	C
PIRA	3	0.37	1.11	0.23	C	0.41	0.08	B	0.95	0.12	C	0.39	0.05	C
PIRA	4	0.37	1.25	0.17	C	0.46	0.06	B	0.80	0.12	C	0.37	0.06	C
PIRE	1	0.41	1.48	0.04	B	0.61	0.02	A	0.82	0.19	B	0.50	0.05	C
PIRE	2	0.41	1.23	0.05	A	0.50	0.01	A	0.82	0.03	A	0.41	0.02	A
PIRE	3	0.41	1.11	0.23	C	0.45	0.09	B	0.85	0.02	A	0.38	0.06	A
PIRE	4	0.41	1.25	0.17	C	0.51	0.07	B	0.73	0.06	A	0.37	0.02	A
PIRI	1	0.47	1.47	0.31	C	0.69	0.14	B	0.82	0.19	C	0.57	0.11	C
PIRI	2	0.47	1.22	0.18	C	0.57	0.09	B	1.03	0.13	C	0.59	0.06	C
PIRI	3	0.47	1.11	0.23	C	0.52	0.11	B	0.95	0.12	C	0.50	0.07	C
PIRI	4	0.47	1.25	0.17	C	0.59	0.08	B	0.80	0.12	C	0.47	0.08	C
PISA	1	0.37	1.47	0.31	C	0.54	0.11	B	0.82	0.19	C	0.44	0.07	C
PISA	2	0.37	1.22	0.18	C	0.45	0.07	B	1.03	0.13	C	0.46	0.04	C
PISA	3	0.37	1.11	0.23	C	0.41	0.08	B	0.95	0.12	C	0.39	0.05	C
PISA	4	0.37	1.25	0.17	C	0.46	0.06	B	0.80	0.12	C	0.37	0.06	C
PISE	1	0.51	1.47	0.31	C	0.75	0.16	B	0.82	0.19	C	0.62	0.13	C
PISE	2	0.51	1.22	0.18	C	0.62	0.09	B	1.03	0.13	C	0.64	0.06	C

(Appendix 4 continued on next page)

(Appendix 4 continued)

Species code	Size class	Bole init density	Branch-bole ratio	Uncert B-B ratio	Uncert_bb ratio code	FWD initial density	Uncert FWD density	Uncert FWD code	Relative density	Uncert Rel density	Uncert Rel Den code	Decayed density	Uncert Decayed density	Uncert Decayed code
PISE	3	0.51	1.11	0.23	C	0.56	0.12	B	0.95	0.12	C	0.53	0.07	C
PISE	4	0.51	1.25	0.17	C	0.64	0.09	B	0.80	0.12	C	0.51	0.08	C
PIST2	1	0.35	1.47	0.31	C	0.51	0.11	B	0.82	0.19	C	0.42	0.07	C
PIST2	2	0.35	1.22	0.18	C	0.43	0.06	B	1.03	0.13	C	0.44	0.04	C
PIST2	3	0.35	1.11	0.23	C	0.39	0.08	B	0.95	0.12	C	0.37	0.04	C
PIST2	4	0.35	1.25	0.17	C	0.44	0.06	B	0.80	0.12	C	0.35	0.06	C
PIST	1	0.34	1.47	0.31	C	0.50	0.10	B	0.82	0.19	C	0.41	0.07	C
PIST	2	0.34	1.22	0.18	C	0.41	0.06	B	1.03	0.13	C	0.42	0.04	C
PIST	3	0.34	1.11	0.23	C	0.38	0.08	B	0.95	0.12	C	0.36	0.04	C
PIST	4	0.34	1.25	0.17	C	0.43	0.06	B	0.80	0.12	C	0.34	0.06	C
PISY	1	0.41	1.47	0.31	C	0.60	0.13	B	0.82	0.19	C	0.49	0.09	C
PISY	2	0.41	1.22	0.18	C	0.50	0.08	B	1.03	0.13	C	0.51	0.05	C
PISY	3	0.41	1.11	0.23	C	0.45	0.09	B	0.95	0.12	C	0.43	0.05	C
PISY	4	0.41	1.25	0.17	C	0.51	0.07	B	0.80	0.12	C	0.41	0.07	C
PITA	1	0.47	1.07	0.03	B	0.51	0.02	A	0.82	0.19	C	0.42	0.05	C
PITA	2	0.47	1.04	0.03	B	0.49	0.01	A	1.03	0.13	C	0.50	0.03	C
PITA	3	0.47	1.00	0.01	B	0.47	0.00	A	0.95	0.12	C	0.45	0.03	C
PITA	4	0.47	1.04	0.02	B	0.49	0.01	A	0.80	0.12	C	0.39	0.06	C
PIVI	1	0.45	1.47	0.31	C	0.66	0.14	B	0.82	0.19	C	0.54	0.10	C
PIVI	2	0.45	1.22	0.18	C	0.55	0.08	B	1.03	0.13	C	0.56	0.05	C
PIVI	3	0.45	1.11	0.23	C	0.50	0.10	B	0.95	0.12	C	0.48	0.06	C
PIVI	4	0.45	1.25	0.17	C	0.56	0.08	B	0.80	0.12	C	0.45	0.07	C
PLAQ	1	0.53	1.47	0.31	C	0.78	0.16	B	0.83	0.10	C	0.65	0.13	C
PLAQ	2	0.53	1.22	0.18	C	0.65	0.10	B	0.85	0.15	C	0.55	0.07	C
PLAQ	3	0.53	1.11	0.23	C	0.59	0.12	B	0.92	0.14	C	0.54	0.08	C
PLAQ	4	0.53	1.25	0.17	C	0.66	0.09	B	0.71	0.12	C	0.47	0.07	C
PLOC	1	0.46	1.47	0.31	C	0.68	0.14	B	0.83	0.10	C	0.56	0.10	C
PLOC	2	0.46	1.22	0.18	C	0.56	0.08	B	0.85	0.15	C	0.48	0.05	C
PLOC	3	0.46	1.11	0.23	C	0.51	0.10	B	0.92	0.14	C	0.47	0.06	C
PLOC	4	0.46	1.25	0.17	C	0.58	0.08	B	0.71	0.12	C	0.41	0.06	C
POAL	1	0.37	1.47	0.31	C	0.54	0.11	B	0.83	0.10	C	0.45	0.07	C
POAL	2	0.37	1.22	0.18	C	0.45	0.07	B	0.85	0.15	C	0.38	0.04	C
POAL	3	0.37	1.11	0.23	C	0.41	0.08	B	0.92	0.14	C	0.38	0.05	C
POAL	4	0.37	1.25	0.17	C	0.46	0.06	B	0.71	0.12	C	0.33	0.05	C
POAN	1	0.34	1.47	0.31	C	0.50	0.10	B	0.83	0.10	C	0.41	0.06	C
POAN	2	0.34	1.22	0.18	C	0.41	0.06	B	0.85	0.15	C	0.35	0.04	C
POAN	3	0.34	1.11	0.23	C	0.38	0.08	B	0.92	0.14	C	0.35	0.05	C
POAN	4	0.34	1.25	0.17	C	0.43	0.06	B	0.71	0.12	C	0.31	0.05	C
POBA	1	0.31	1.47	0.31	C	0.46	0.09	B	0.98	0.03	A	0.45	0.04	B
POBA	2	0.31	1.22	0.18	C	0.38	0.06	B	1.04	0.01	A	0.39	0.04	B
POBA	3	0.31	1.11	0.23	C	0.34	0.07	B	1.04	0.01	A	0.36	0.03	B

Species code	Size class	Bole init density	Branch-bole ratio	Uncert B-B ratio	Uncert_bb ratio code	FWD initial density	Uncert FWD density	Uncert FWD code	Relative density	Uncert Rel density	Uncert Rel Den code	Decayed density	Uncert Decayed density	Uncert Decayed code
POBA	4	0.31	1.25	0.17	C	0.39	0.05	B	0.71	0.12	C	0.28	0.05	C
PODE	1	0.37	1.47	0.31	C	0.54	0.11	B	0.83	0.10	C	0.45	0.07	C
PODE	2	0.37	1.22	0.18	C	0.45	0.07	B	0.85	0.15	C	0.38	0.04	C
PODE	3	0.37	1.11	0.23	C	0.41	0.08	B	0.92	0.14	C	0.38	0.05	C
PODE	4	0.37	1.25	0.17	C	0.46	0.06	B	0.71	0.12	C	0.33	0.05	C
POFR	1	0.34	1.47	0.31	C	0.50	0.10	B	0.83	0.10	C	0.41	0.06	C
POFR	2	0.34	1.22	0.18	C	0.41	0.06	B	0.85	0.15	C	0.35	0.04	C
POFR	3	0.34	1.11	0.23	C	0.38	0.08	B	0.92	0.14	C	0.35	0.05	C
POFR	4	0.34	1.25	0.17	C	0.43	0.06	B	0.71	0.10	C	0.31	0.05	C
POGR	1	0.36	1.47	0.31	C	0.53	0.11	B	0.83	0.10	C	0.44	0.07	C
POGR	2	0.36	1.22	0.18	C	0.44	0.07	B	0.85	0.15	C	0.38	0.04	C
POGR	3	0.36	1.11	0.23	C	0.40	0.08	B	0.92	0.14	C	0.37	0.05	C
POGR	4	0.36	1.25	0.17	C	0.45	0.06	B	0.71	0.10	C	0.32	0.05	C
POHE	1	0.37	1.47	0.31	C	0.54	0.11	B	0.83	0.10	C	0.45	0.07	C
POHE	2	0.37	1.22	0.18	C	0.45	0.07	B	0.85	0.15	C	0.38	0.04	C
POHE	3	0.37	1.11	0.23	C	0.41	0.08	B	0.92	0.14	C	0.38	0.05	C
POHE	4	0.37	1.25	0.17	C	0.46	0.06	B	0.71	0.12	C	0.33	0.05	C
POSA	1	0.37	1.47	0.31	C	0.54	0.11	B	0.83	0.10	C	0.45	0.07	C
POSA	2	0.37	1.22	0.18	C	0.45	0.07	B	0.85	0.15	C	0.38	0.04	C
POSA	3	0.37	1.11	0.23	C	0.41	0.08	B	0.92	0.14	C	0.38	0.05	C
POSA	4	0.37	1.25	0.17	C	0.46	0.06	B	0.71	0.12	C	0.33	0.05	C
POSP	1	0.37	1.47	0.31	C	0.54	0.11	B	0.89	0.08	B	0.48	0.04	B
POSP	2	0.37	1.22	0.18	C	0.45	0.07	B	0.92	0.02	A	0.41	0.04	B
POSP	3	0.37	1.11	0.23	C	0.41	0.08	B	0.93	0.09	B	0.38	0.04	B
POSP	4	0.37	1.25	0.17	C	0.46	0.06	B	0.71	0.12	C	0.33	0.05	C
POTR	1	0.35	1.60	0.07	A	0.56	0.02	A	0.88	0.01	A	0.49	0.05	B
POTR	2	0.35	1.27	0.05	A	0.45	0.02	A	0.91	0.01	A	0.41	0.04	B
POTR	3	0.35	1.08	0.01	B	0.38	0.00	A	1.01	0.01	A	0.38	0.04	B
POTR	4	0.35	1.22	0.01	B	0.43	0.00	A	0.71	0.12	C	0.31	0.04	C
PRSP	1	0.58	1.47	0.31	C	0.85	0.18	B	0.83	0.10	C	0.70	0.16	C
PRSP	2	0.58	1.22	0.18	C	0.71	0.11	B	0.85	0.15	C	0.61	0.08	C
PRSP	3	0.58	1.11	0.23	C	0.64	0.13	B	0.92	0.14	C	0.59	0.09	C
PRSP	4	0.58	1.25	0.17	C	0.73	0.10	B	0.71	0.12	C	0.52	0.08	C
PRAM	1	0.47	1.47	0.31	C	0.69	0.14	B	0.83	0.10	C	0.57	0.10	C
PRAM	2	0.47	1.22	0.18	C	0.57	0.09	B	0.85	0.15	C	0.49	0.06	C
PRAM	3	0.47	1.11	0.23	C	0.52	0.11	B	0.92	0.14	C	0.48	0.07	C
PRAM	4	0.47	1.25	0.17	C	0.59	0.08	B	0.71	0.12	C	0.42	0.06	C
PRNI	1	0.47	1.47	0.31	C	0.69	0.14	B	0.83	0.10	C	0.57	0.10	C
PRNI	2	0.47	1.22	0.18	C	0.57	0.09	B	0.85	0.15	C	0.49	0.06	C
PRNI	3	0.47	1.11	0.23	C	0.52	0.11	B	0.92	0.14	C	0.48	0.07	C
PRNI	4	0.47	1.25	0.17	C	0.59	0.08	B	0.71	0.12	C	0.42	0.06	C

(Appendix 4 continued on next page)

(Appendix 4 continued)

Species code	Size class	Bole init density	Branch-bole ratio	Uncert B-B ratio	Uncert_bb ratio code	FWD initial density	Uncert FWD density	Uncert FWD code	Relative density	Uncert Rel density	Uncert Rel Den code	Decayed density	Uncert Decayed density	Uncert Decayed code
PRPE	1	0.36	1.47	0.31	C	0.53	0.11	B	0.83	0.10	C	0.44	0.07	C
PRPE	2	0.36	1.22	0.18	C	0.44	0.07	B	0.85	0.15	C	0.38	0.04	C
PRPE	3	0.36	1.11	0.23	C	0.40	0.08	B	0.92	0.14	C	0.37	0.05	C
PRPE	4	0.36	1.25	0.17	C	0.45	0.06	B	0.71	0.12	C	0.32	0.05	C
PRSE	1	0.47	1.47	0.31	C	0.69	0.14	B	0.83	0.10	C	0.57	0.10	C
PRSE	2	0.47	1.22	0.18	C	0.57	0.09	B	0.85	0.15	C	0.49	0.06	C
PRSE	3	0.47	1.11	0.23	C	0.52	0.11	B	0.92	0.14	C	0.48	0.07	C
PRSE	4	0.47	1.25	0.17	C	0.59	0.08	B	0.71	0.12	C	0.42	0.06	C
PRSP2	1	0.47	1.47	0.31	C	0.69	0.14	B	0.83	0.10	C	0.57	0.10	C
PRSP2	2	0.47	1.22	0.18	C	0.57	0.09	B	0.85	0.15	C	0.49	0.06	C
PRSP2	3	0.47	1.11	0.23	C	0.52	0.11	B	0.92	0.14	C	0.48	0.07	C
PRSP2	4	0.47	1.25	0.17	C	0.59	0.08	B	0.71	0.12	C	0.42	0.06	C
PRVI	1	0.36	1.47	0.31	C	0.53	0.11	B	0.83	0.10	C	0.44	0.07	C
PRVI	2	0.36	1.22	0.18	C	0.44	0.07	B	0.85	0.15	C	0.38	0.04	C
PRVI	3	0.36	1.11	0.23	C	0.40	0.08	B	0.92	0.14	C	0.37	0.05	C
PRVI	4	0.36	1.25	0.17	C	0.45	0.06	B	0.71	0.12	C	0.32	0.05	C
PSME	1	0.45	1.41	0.02	B	0.64	0.01	A	0.90	0.02	A	0.57	0.05	B
PSME	2	0.45	1.20	0.03	A	0.54	0.01	A	0.99	0.03	A	0.54	0.04	A
PSME	3	0.45	1.05	0.03	A	0.47	0.01	A	0.80	0.02	A	0.38	0.02	A
PSME	4	0.45	1.26	0.01	B	0.57	0.00	A	0.75	0.07	B	0.43	0.04	B
QUAG	1	0.70	1.47	0.31	C	1.03	0.21	B	0.83	0.10	C	0.85	0.22	C
QUAG	2	0.70	1.22	0.18	C	0.85	0.13	B	0.85	0.15	C	0.72	0.11	C
QUAG	3	0.70	1.11	0.23	C	0.78	0.16	B	0.92	0.14	C	0.72	0.13	C
QUAG	4	0.70	1.25	0.17	C	0.88	0.12	B	0.71	0.12	C	0.63	0.11	C
QUAL	1	0.60	1.11	0.02	B	0.75	0.01	A	0.83	0.10	C	0.62	0.03	C
QUAL	2	0.60	0.96	0.01	B	0.66	0.01	A	0.85	0.15	C	0.56	0.03	C
QUAL	3	0.60	1.10	0.01	B	0.57	0.01	A	0.92	0.14	C	0.52	0.04	C
QUAL	4	0.60	1.47	0.31	C	0.66	0.01	A	0.71	0.12	C	0.47	0.04	C
QUAR	1	0.70	1.47	0.31	C	1.03	0.21	B	0.83	0.10	C	0.85	0.22	C
QUAR	2	0.70	1.22	0.18	C	0.85	0.13	B	0.85	0.15	C	0.72	0.11	C
QUAR	3	0.70	1.11	0.23	C	0.78	0.16	B	0.92	0.14	C	0.72	0.13	C
QUAR	4	0.70	1.25	0.17	C	0.88	0.12	B	0.71	0.12	C	0.63	0.11	C
QUBI	1	0.64	1.47	0.31	C	0.94	0.20	B	0.83	0.10	C	0.78	0.19	C
QUBI	2	0.64	1.22	0.18	C	0.78	0.12	B	0.85	0.15	C	0.66	0.10	C
QUBI	3	0.64	1.11	0.23	C	0.71	0.15	B	0.92	0.14	C	0.65	0.11	C
QUBI	4	0.64	1.25	0.17	C	0.80	0.11	B	0.71	0.12	C	0.57	0.10	C
QUCH	1	0.70	1.47	0.31	C	1.03	0.21	B	0.83	0.10	C	0.85	0.22	C
QUCH	2	0.70	1.22	0.18	C	0.85	0.13	B	0.85	0.15	C	0.72	0.11	C
QUCH	3	0.70	1.11	0.23	C	0.78	0.16	B	0.92	0.14	C	0.72	0.13	C
QUCH	4	0.70	1.25	0.17	C	0.88	0.12	B	0.71	0.12	C	0.63	0.11	C
QUCO	1	0.60	1.47	0.31	C	0.88	0.18	B	0.83	0.10	C	0.73	0.16	C

Species code	Size class	Bole init density	Branch-bole ratio	Uncert B-B ratio	Uncert_bb ratio code	FWD initial density	Uncert FWD density	Uncert FWD code	Relative density	Uncert Rel density	Uncert Rel Den code	Decayed density	Uncert Decayed density	Uncert Decayed code
QUCO	2	0.60	1.22	0.18	C	0.73	0.11	B	0.85	0.15	C	0.62	0.09	C
QUCO	3	0.60	1.11	0.23	C	0.66	0.14	B	0.92	0.14	C	0.61	0.10	C
QUCO	4	0.60	1.25	0.17	C	0.75	0.10	B	0.71	0.12	C	0.54	0.09	C
QUDO	1	0.51	1.47	0.31	C	0.75	0.16	B	0.83	0.10	C	0.62	0.12	C
QUDO	2	0.51	1.22	0.18	C	0.62	0.09	B	0.85	0.15	C	0.53	0.06	C
QUDO	3	0.51	1.11	0.23	C	0.56	0.12	B	0.92	0.14	C	0.51	0.08	C
QUDO	4	0.51	1.25	0.17	C	0.64	0.09	B	0.71	0.12	C	0.46	0.07	C
QUDU	1	0.60	1.47	0.31	C	0.88	0.18	B	0.83	0.10	C	0.73	0.16	C
QUDU	2	0.60	1.22	0.18	C	0.73	0.11	B	0.85	0.15	C	0.62	0.09	C
QUDU	3	0.60	1.11	0.23	C	0.66	0.14	B	0.92	0.14	C	0.61	0.10	C
QUDU	4	0.60	1.25	0.17	C	0.75	0.10	B	0.71	0.12	C	0.54	0.09	C
QUEL	1	0.56	1.47	0.31	C	0.82	0.17	B	0.83	0.10	C	0.68	0.14	C
QUEL	2	0.56	1.22	0.18	C	0.68	0.10	B	0.85	0.15	C	0.58	0.07	C
QUEL	3	0.56	1.11	0.23	C	0.62	0.13	B	0.92	0.14	C	0.57	0.09	C
QUEL	4	0.56	1.25	0.17	C	0.70	0.10	B	0.71	0.12	C	0.50	0.08	C
QUEM	1	0.70	1.47	0.31	C	1.03	0.21	B	0.83	0.10	C	0.85	0.22	C
QUEM	2	0.70	1.22	0.18	C	0.85	0.13	B	0.85	0.15	C	0.72	0.11	C
QUEM	3	0.70	1.11	0.23	C	0.78	0.16	B	0.92	0.14	C	0.72	0.13	C
QUEM	4	0.70	1.25	0.17	C	0.88	0.12	B	0.71	0.12	C	0.63	0.11	C
QUEN	1	0.70	1.47	0.31	C	1.03	0.21	B	0.83	0.10	C	0.85	0.22	C
QUEN	2	0.70	1.22	0.18	C	0.85	0.13	B	0.85	0.15	C	0.72	0.11	C
QUEN	3	0.70	1.11	0.23	C	0.78	0.16	B	0.92	0.14	C	0.72	0.13	C
QUEN	4	0.70	1.25	0.17	C	0.88	0.12	B	0.71	0.12	C	0.63	0.11	C
QUFA	1	0.52	1.47	0.31	C	0.76	0.16	B	0.83	0.10	C	0.63	0.13	C
QUFA	2	0.52	1.22	0.18	C	0.63	0.10	B	0.85	0.15	C	0.54	0.07	C
QUFA	3	0.52	1.11	0.23	C	0.58	0.12	B	0.92	0.14	C	0.53	0.08	C
QUFA	4	0.52	1.25	0.17	C	0.65	0.09	B	0.71	0.12	C	0.46	0.07	C
QUFA2	1	0.61	1.47	0.31	C	0.90	0.19	B	0.83	0.10	C	0.75	0.17	C
QUFA2	2	0.61	1.22	0.18	C	0.74	0.11	B	0.85	0.15	C	0.63	0.09	C
QUFA2	3	0.61	1.11	0.23	C	0.68	0.14	B	0.92	0.14	C	0.62	0.10	C
QUFA2	4	0.61	1.25	0.17	C	0.76	0.11	B	0.71	0.12	C	0.54	0.09	C
QUGA2	1	0.64	1.47	0.31	C	0.94	0.20	B	0.83	0.10	C	0.78	0.19	C
QUGA2	2	0.64	1.22	0.18	C	0.78	0.12	B	0.85	0.15	C	0.66	0.10	C
QUGA2	3	0.64	1.11	0.23	C	0.71	0.15	B	0.92	0.14	C	0.65	0.11	C
QUGA2	4	0.64	1.25	0.17	C	0.80	0.11	B	0.71	0.12	C	0.57	0.10	C
QUGA	1	0.64	1.31	0.04	B	0.84	0.03	A	0.83	0.10	C	0.70	0.04	C
QUGA	2	0.64	1.07	0.02	B	0.69	0.01	A	0.85	0.15	C	0.59	0.03	C
QUGA	3	0.64	0.93	0.02	B	0.59	0.01	A	0.92	0.14	C	0.54	0.04	C
QUGA	4	0.64	1.09	0.02	B	0.70	0.01	A	0.71	0.12	C	0.50	0.04	C
QUHY	1	0.70	1.47	0.31	C	1.03	0.21	B	0.83	0.10	C	0.85	0.22	C
QUHY	2	0.70	1.22	0.18	C	0.85	0.13	B	0.85	0.15	C	0.72	0.11	C

(Appendix 4 continued on next page)

(Appendix 4 continued)

Species code	Size class	Bole init density	Branch-bole ratio	Uncert B-B ratio	Uncert_bb ratio code	FWD initial density	Uncert FWD density	Uncert FWD code	Relative density	Uncert Rel density	Uncert Rel Den code	Decayed density	Uncert Decayed density	Uncert Decayed code
QUHY	3	0.70	1.11	0.23	C	0.78	0.16	B	0.92	0.14	C	0.72	0.13	C
QUHY	4	0.70	1.25	0.17	C	0.88	0.12	B	0.71	0.12	C	0.63	0.11	C
QUIL	1	0.56	1.47	0.31	C	0.82	0.17	B	0.83	0.10	C	0.68	0.14	C
QUIL	2	0.56	1.22	0.18	C	0.68	0.10	B	0.85	0.15	C	0.58	0.07	C
QUIL	3	0.56	1.11	0.23	C	0.62	0.13	B	0.92	0.14	C	0.57	0.09	C
QUIL	4	0.56	1.25	0.17	C	0.70	0.10	B	0.71	0.12	C	0.50	0.08	C
QUIM	1	0.56	1.47	0.31	C	0.82	0.17	B	0.83	0.10	C	0.68	0.14	C
QUIM	2	0.56	1.22	0.18	C	0.68	0.10	B	0.85	0.15	C	0.58	0.07	C
QUIM	3	0.56	1.11	0.23	C	0.62	0.13	B	0.92	0.14	C	0.57	0.09	C
QUIM	4	0.56	1.25	0.17	C	0.70	0.10	B	0.71	0.12	C	0.50	0.08	C
QUIN	1	0.56	1.47	0.31	C	0.82	0.17	B	0.83	0.10	C	0.68	0.14	C
QUIN	2	0.56	1.22	0.18	C	0.68	0.10	B	0.85	0.15	C	0.58	0.07	C
QUIN	3	0.56	1.11	0.23	C	0.62	0.13	B	0.92	0.14	C	0.57	0.09	C
QUIN	4	0.56	1.25	0.17	C	0.70	0.10	B	0.71	0.12	C	0.50	0.08	C
QUKE	1	0.51	1.47	0.31	C	0.75	0.16	B	0.83	0.10	C	0.62	0.12	C
QUKE	2	0.51	1.22	0.18	C	0.62	0.09	B	0.85	0.15	C	0.53	0.06	C
QUKE	3	0.51	1.11	0.23	C	0.56	0.12	B	0.92	0.14	C	0.51	0.08	C
QUKE	4	0.51	1.25	0.17	C	0.64	0.09	B	0.71	0.12	C	0.46	0.07	C
QULA	1	0.52	1.47	0.31	C	0.76	0.16	B	0.83	0.10	C	0.63	0.13	C
QULA	2	0.52	1.22	0.18	C	0.63	0.10	B	0.85	0.15	C	0.54	0.07	C
QULA	3	0.52	1.11	0.23	C	0.58	0.12	B	0.92	0.14	C	0.53	0.08	C
QULA	4	0.52	1.25	0.17	C	0.65	0.09	B	0.71	0.12	C	0.46	0.07	C
QULA2	1	0.56	1.47	0.31	C	0.82	0.17	B	0.83	0.10	C	0.68	0.14	C
QULA2	2	0.56	1.22	0.18	C	0.68	0.10	B	0.85	0.15	C	0.58	0.07	C
QULA2	3	0.56	1.11	0.23	C	0.62	0.13	B	0.92	0.14	C	0.57	0.09	C
QULA2	4	0.56	1.25	0.17	C	0.70	0.10	B	0.71	0.12	C	0.50	0.08	C
QULO	1	0.64	1.47	0.31	C	0.94	0.20	B	0.83	0.10	C	0.78	0.19	C
QULO	2	0.64	1.22	0.18	C	0.78	0.12	B	0.85	0.15	C	0.66	0.10	C
QULO	3	0.64	1.11	0.23	C	0.71	0.15	B	0.92	0.14	C	0.65	0.11	C
QULO	4	0.64	1.25	0.17	C	0.80	0.11	B	0.71	0.12	C	0.57	0.10	C
QULY	1	0.57	1.47	0.31	C	0.84	0.17	B	0.83	0.10	C	0.70	0.15	C
QULY	2	0.57	1.22	0.18	C	0.69	0.10	B	0.85	0.15	C	0.59	0.08	C
QULY	3	0.57	1.11	0.23	C	0.63	0.13	B	0.92	0.14	C	0.58	0.09	C
QULY	4	0.57	1.25	0.17	C	0.71	0.10	B	0.71	0.12	C	0.51	0.08	C
QUMA	1	0.58	1.47	0.31	C	0.85	0.18	B	0.83	0.10	C	0.70	0.16	C
QUMA	2	0.58	1.22	0.18	C	0.71	0.11	B	0.85	0.15	C	0.61	0.08	C
QUMA	3	0.58	1.11	0.23	C	0.64	0.13	B	0.92	0.14	C	0.59	0.09	C
QUMA	4	0.58	1.25	0.17	C	0.73	0.10	B	0.71	0.12	C	0.52	0.08	C
QUMA2	1	0.56	1.47	0.31	C	0.82	0.17	B	0.83	0.10	C	0.68	0.14	C
QUMA2	2	0.56	1.22	0.18	C	0.68	0.10	B	0.85	0.15	C	0.58	0.07	C
QUMA2	3	0.56	1.11	0.23	C	0.62	0.13	B	0.92	0.14	C	0.57	0.09	C

Species code	Size class	Bole init density	Branch-bole ratio	Uncert B-B ratio	Uncert_bb ratio code	FWD initial density	Uncert FWD density	Uncert FWD code	Relative density	Uncert Rel density	Uncert Rel Den code	Decayed density	Uncert Decayed density	Uncert Decayed code
QUMA2	4	0.56	1.25	0.17	C	0.70	0.10	B	0.71	0.12	C	0.50	0.08	C
QUMI	1	0.60	1.47	0.31	C	0.88	0.18	B	0.83	0.10	C	0.73	0.16	C
QUMI	2	0.60	1.22	0.18	C	0.73	0.11	B	0.85	0.15	C	0.62	0.09	C
QUMI	3	0.60	1.11	0.23	C	0.66	0.14	B	0.92	0.14	C	0.61	0.10	C
QUMI	4	0.60	1.25	0.17	C	0.75	0.10	B	0.71	0.12	C	0.54	0.09	C
QUMU	1	0.60	1.47	0.31	C	0.88	0.18	B	0.83	0.10	C	0.73	0.16	C
QUMU	2	0.60	1.22	0.18	C	0.73	0.11	B	0.85	0.15	C	0.62	0.09	C
QUMU	3	0.60	1.11	0.23	C	0.66	0.14	B	0.92	0.14	C	0.61	0.10	C
QUMU	4	0.60	1.25	0.17	C	0.75	0.10	B	0.71	0.12	C	0.54	0.09	C
QUNI	1	0.56	1.47	0.31	C	0.82	0.17	B	0.83	0.10	C	0.68	0.14	C
QUNI	2	0.56	1.22	0.18	C	0.68	0.10	B	0.85	0.15	C	0.58	0.07	C
QUNI	3	0.56	1.11	0.23	C	0.62	0.13	B	0.92	0.14	C	0.57	0.09	C
QUNI	4	0.56	1.25	0.17	C	0.70	0.10	B	0.71	0.12	C	0.50	0.08	C
QUNU	1	0.56	1.47	0.31	C	0.82	0.17	B	0.83	0.10	C	0.68	0.14	C
QUNU	2	0.56	1.22	0.18	C	0.68	0.10	B	0.85	0.15	C	0.58	0.07	C
QUNU	3	0.56	1.11	0.23	C	0.62	0.13	B	0.92	0.14	C	0.57	0.09	C
QUNU	4	0.56	1.25	0.17	C	0.70	0.10	B	0.71	0.12	C	0.50	0.08	C
QUOB	1	0.70	1.47	0.31	C	1.03	0.21	B	0.83	0.10	C	0.85	0.22	C
QUOB	2	0.70	1.22	0.18	C	0.85	0.13	B	0.85	0.15	C	0.72	0.11	C
QUOB	3	0.70	1.11	0.23	C	0.78	0.16	B	0.92	0.14	C	0.72	0.13	C
QUOB	4	0.70	1.25	0.17	C	0.88	0.12	B	0.71	0.12	C	0.63	0.11	C
QUPA	1	0.58	1.47	0.31	C	0.85	0.18	B	0.83	0.10	C	0.70	0.16	C
QUPA	2	0.58	1.22	0.18	C	0.71	0.11	B	0.85	0.15	C	0.61	0.08	C
QUPA	3	0.58	1.11	0.23	C	0.64	0.13	B	0.92	0.14	C	0.59	0.09	C
QUPA	4	0.58	1.25	0.17	C	0.73	0.10	B	0.71	0.12	C	0.52	0.08	C
QUPH	1	0.56	1.47	0.31	C	0.82	0.17	B	0.83	0.10	C	0.68	0.14	C
QUPH	2	0.56	1.22	0.18	C	0.68	0.10	B	0.85	0.15	C	0.58	0.07	C
QUPH	3	0.56	1.11	0.23	C	0.62	0.13	B	0.92	0.14	C	0.57	0.09	C
QUPH	4	0.56	1.25	0.17	C	0.70	0.10	B	0.71	0.12	C	0.50	0.08	C
QUPR	1	0.57	1.47	0.31	C	0.84	0.17	B	0.83	0.10	C	0.70	0.15	C
QUPR	2	0.57	1.22	0.18	C	0.69	0.10	B	0.85	0.15	C	0.59	0.08	C
QUPR	3	0.57	1.11	0.23	C	0.63	0.13	B	0.92	0.14	C	0.58	0.09	C
QUPR	4	0.57	1.25	0.17	C	0.71	0.10	B	0.71	0.12	C	0.51	0.08	C
QURU	1	0.56	1.29	0.03	B	0.72	0.01	A	0.83	0.10	C	0.60	0.03	C
QURU	2	0.56	1.14	0.03	B	0.64	0.02	A	0.85	0.15	C	0.55	0.03	C
QURU	3	0.56	1.10	0.02	B	0.61	0.01	A	0.92	0.14	C	0.56	0.04	C
QURU	4	0.56	1.16	0.02	B	0.65	0.01	A	0.71	0.12	C	0.46	0.04	C
QUSH	1	0.56	1.47	0.31	C	0.82	0.17	B	0.83	0.10	C	0.68	0.14	C
QUSH	2	0.56	1.22	0.18	C	0.68	0.10	B	0.85	0.15	C	0.58	0.07	C
QUSH	3	0.56	1.11	0.23	C	0.62	0.13	B	0.92	0.14	C	0.57	0.09	C
QUSH	4	0.56	1.25	0.17	C	0.70	0.10	B	0.71	0.12	C	0.50	0.08	C

(Appendix 4 continued on next page)

(Appendix 4 continued)

Species code	Size class	Bole init density	Branch-bole ratio	Uncert B-B ratio	Uncert_bb ratio code	FWD initial density	Uncert FWD density	Uncert FWD code	Relative density	Uncert Rel density	Uncert Rel Den code	Decayed density	Uncert Decayed density	Uncert Decayed code
QUSP	1	0.58	1.47	0.31	C	0.85	0.18	B	0.83	0.10	C	0.70	0.16	C
QUSP	2	0.58	1.22	0.18	C	0.71	0.11	B	0.61	0.04	A	0.43	0.02	A
QUSP	3	0.58	1.11	0.23	C	0.64	0.13	B	0.59	0.07	A	0.38	0.04	A
QUSP	4	0.58	1.25	0.17	C	0.73	0.10	B	0.56	0.04	A	0.41	0.02	A
QUST	1	0.60	1.47	0.31	C	0.88	0.18	B	0.83	0.10	C	0.73	0.16	C
QUST	2	0.60	1.22	0.18	C	0.73	0.11	B	0.85	0.15	C	0.62	0.09	C
QUST	3	0.60	1.11	0.23	C	0.66	0.14	B	0.92	0.14	C	0.61	0.10	C
QUST	4	0.60	1.25	0.17	C	0.75	0.10	B	0.71	0.12	C	0.54	0.09	C
QUVE	1	0.56	1.47	0.31	C	0.82	0.17	B	0.83	0.10	C	0.68	0.14	C
QUVE	2	0.56	1.22	0.18	C	0.68	0.10	B	0.85	0.15	C	0.58	0.07	C
QUVE	3	0.56	1.11	0.23	C	0.62	0.13	B	0.92	0.14	C	0.57	0.09	C
QUVE	4	0.56	1.25	0.17	C	0.70	0.10	B	0.71	0.12	C	0.50	0.08	C
QUVI	1	0.80	1.47	0.31	C	1.18	0.24	B	0.83	0.10	C	0.98	0.28	C
QUVI	2	0.80	1.22	0.18	C	0.97	0.15	B	0.85	0.15	C	0.83	0.15	C
QUVI	3	0.80	1.11	0.23	C	0.89	0.18	B	0.92	0.14	C	0.82	0.16	C
QUVI	4	0.80	1.25	0.17	C	1.00	0.14	B	0.71	0.12	C	0.71	0.15	C
QUWI	1	0.70	1.47	0.31	C	1.03	0.21	B	0.83	0.10	C	0.85	0.22	C
QUWI	2	0.70	1.22	0.18	C	0.85	0.13	B	0.85	0.15	C	0.72	0.11	C
QUWI	3	0.70	1.11	0.23	C	0.78	0.16	B	0.92	0.14	C	0.72	0.13	C
QUWI	4	0.70	1.25	0.17	C	0.88	0.12	B	0.71	0.12	C	0.63	0.11	C
RONE	1	0.66	1.47	0.31	C	0.97	0.20	B	0.83	0.10	C	0.80	0.20	C
RONE	2	0.66	1.22	0.18	C	0.80	0.12	B	0.85	0.15	C	0.68	0.10	C
RONE	3	0.66	1.11	0.23	C	0.73	0.15	B	0.92	0.14	C	0.67	0.11	C
RONE	4	0.66	1.25	0.17	C	0.83	0.11	B	0.71	0.12	C	0.59	0.10	C
ROPS	1	0.66	1.47	0.31	C	0.97	0.20	B	0.83	0.10	C	0.80	0.20	C
ROPS	2	0.66	1.22	0.18	C	0.80	0.12	B	0.85	0.15	C	0.68	0.10	C
ROPS	3	0.66	1.11	0.23	C	0.73	0.11	B	0.92	0.14	C	0.67	0.11	C
ROPS	4	0.66	1.25	0.17	C	0.83	0.11	B	0.71	0.12	C	0.59	0.10	C
SASP2	1	0.36	1.47	0.31	C	0.53	0.11	B	0.83	0.10	C	0.44	0.07	C
SASP2	2	0.36	1.22	0.18	C	0.44	0.07	B	0.85	0.15	C	0.38	0.04	C
SASP2	3	0.36	1.11	0.23	C	0.40	0.08	B	0.92	0.14	C	0.37	0.05	C
SASP2	4	0.36	1.25	0.17	C	0.45	0.06	B	0.71	0.12	C	0.32	0.05	C
SASE	1	0.47	1.47	0.31	C	0.69	0.14	B	0.83	0.10	C	0.57	0.10	C
SASE	2	0.47	1.22	0.18	C	0.57	0.09	B	0.85	0.15	C	0.49	0.06	C
SASE	3	0.47	1.11	0.23	C	0.52	0.11	B	0.92	0.14	C	0.48	0.07	C
SASE	4	0.47	1.25	0.17	C	0.59	0.08	B	0.71	0.12	C	0.42	0.06	C
SAAL	1	0.42	1.24	0.06	B	0.52	0.03	A	0.83	0.10	C	0.43	0.03	C
SAAL	2	0.42	1.19	0.03	B	0.50	0.01	A	0.85	0.15	C	0.43	0.03	C
SAAL	3	0.42	0.91	0.02	B	0.38	0.01	A	0.92	0.14	C	0.35	0.04	C
SAAL	4	0.42	1.11	0.03	B	0.47	0.01	A	0.71	0.12	C	0.34	0.04	C
SESE	1	0.34	1.47	0.31	C	0.50	0.10	B	0.82	0.19	C	0.41	0.07	C

Species code	Size class	Bole init density	Branch-bole ratio	Uncert B-B ratio	Uncert_bb ratio code	FWD initial density	Uncert FWD density	Uncert FWD code	Relative density	Uncert Rel density	Uncert Rel Den code	Decayed density	Uncert Decayed density	Uncert Decayed code
SESE	2	0.34	1.22	0.18	C	0.41	0.06	B	1.03	0.13	C	0.42	0.04	C
SESE	3	0.34	1.11	0.23	C	0.38	0.08	B	0.95	0.12	C	0.36	0.04	C
SESE	4	0.34	1.25	0.17	C	0.43	0.06	B	0.80	0.12	C	0.34	0.06	C
SEGI	1	0.34	1.47	0.31	C	0.50	0.10	B	0.82	0.19	C	0.41	0.07	C
SEGI	2	0.34	1.22	0.18	C	0.41	0.06	B	1.03	0.13	C	0.42	0.04	C
SEGI	3	0.34	1.11	0.23	C	0.38	0.08	B	0.95	0.12	C	0.36	0.04	C
SEGI	4	0.34	1.25	0.17	C	0.43	0.06	B	0.80	0.12	C	0.34	0.06	C
SOFTW	1	0.38	1.47	0.31	C	0.56	0.12	B	0.82	0.19	C	0.46	0.08	C
SOFTW	2	0.38	1.22	0.18	C	0.46	0.07	B	1.03	0.13	C	0.47	0.04	C
SOFTW	3	0.38	1.11	0.23	C	0.42	0.09	B	0.95	0.12	C	0.40	0.05	C
SOFTW	4	0.38	1.25	0.17	C	0.48	0.07	B	0.80	0.12	C	0.38	0.07	C
SOAM	1	0.42	1.47	0.31	C	0.62	0.13	B	0.83	0.10	C	0.51	0.09	C
SOAM	2	0.42	1.22	0.18	C	0.51	0.08	B	0.85	0.15	C	0.43	0.05	C
SOAM	3	0.42	1.11	0.23	C	0.47	0.10	B	0.92	0.14	C	0.43	0.06	C
SOAM	4	0.42	1.25	0.17	C	0.53	0.07	B	0.71	0.12	C	0.38	0.06	C
TASP	1	0.40	1.47	0.31	C	0.59	0.12	B	0.83	0.10	C	0.49	0.08	C
TASP	2	0.40	1.22	0.18	C	0.49	0.07	B	0.85	0.15	C	0.42	0.05	C
TASP	3	0.40	1.11	0.23	C	0.44	0.09	B	0.92	0.14	C	0.40	0.05	C
TASP	4	0.40	1.25	0.17	C	0.50	0.07	B	0.71	0.12	C	0.36	0.06	C
TADI	1	0.42	1.47	0.31	C	0.62	0.13	B	0.83	0.10	C	0.51	0.09	C
TADI	2	0.42	1.22	0.18	C	0.51	0.08	B	0.85	0.15	C	0.43	0.05	C
TADI	3	0.42	1.11	0.23	C	0.47	0.10	B	0.92	0.14	C	0.43	0.06	C
TADI	4	0.42	1.25	0.17	C	0.53	0.07	B	0.71	0.12	C	0.38	0.06	C
TABR	1	0.60	1.47	0.31	C	0.88	0.18	B	0.82	0.19	C	0.73	0.16	C
TABR	2	0.60	1.22	0.18	C	0.73	0.11	B	1.03	0.13	C	0.75	0.08	C
TABR	3	0.60	1.11	0.23	C	0.66	0.14	B	0.95	0.12	C	0.63	0.10	C
TABR	4	0.60	1.25	0.17	C	0.75	0.10	B	0.80	0.12	C	0.60	0.10	C
THOC	1	0.29	1.47	0.31	C	0.43	0.09	B	0.82	0.19	C	0.35	0.06	C
THOC	2	0.29	1.22	0.18	C	0.35	0.05	B	1.03	0.13	C	0.36	0.03	C
THOC	3	0.29	1.11	0.23	C	0.32	0.07	B	0.95	0.12	C	0.31	0.04	C
THOC	4	0.29	1.25	0.17	C	0.36	0.05	B	0.80	0.12	C	0.29	0.06	C
THPL	1	0.31	1.67	0.02	B	0.52	0.01	A	0.92	0.09	B	0.48	0.05	B
THPL	2	0.31	1.60	0.01	B	0.50	0.00	A	1.03	0.13	C	0.51	0.03	C
THPL	3	0.31	1.19	0.02	B	0.37	0.01	A	0.95	0.12	B	0.35	0.03	B
THPL	4	0.31	1.49	0.01	B	0.46	0.00	A	0.72	0.07	C	0.33	0.03	C
TIAM	1	0.32	1.47	0.31	C	0.47	0.10	B	0.83	0.10	C	0.39	0.06	C
TIAM	2	0.32	1.22	0.18	C	0.39	0.06	B	0.85	0.15	C	0.33	0.04	C
TIAM	3	0.32	1.11	0.23	C	0.35	0.07	B	0.92	0.14	C	0.32	0.04	C
TIAM	4	0.32	1.25	0.17	C	0.40	0.06	B	0.71	0.12	C	0.29	0.05	C
TIHE	1	0.32	1.47	0.31	C	0.47	0.10	B	0.83	0.10	C	0.39	0.06	C
TIHE	2	0.32	1.22	0.18	C	0.39	0.06	B	0.85	0.15	C	0.33	0.04	C

(Appendix 4 continued on next page)

(Appendix 4 continued)

Species code	Size class	Bole init density	Branch-bole ratio	Uncert B-B ratio	Uncert_bb ratio code	FWD initial density	Uncert FWD density	Uncert FWD code	Relative density	Uncert Rel density	Uncert Rel Den code	Decayed density	Uncert Decayed density	Uncert Decayed code
TIHE	3	0.32	1.11	0.23	C	0.35	0.07	B	0.92	0.14	C	0.32	0.04	C
TIHE	4	0.32	1.25	0.17	C	0.40	0.06	B	0.71	0.12	C	0.29	0.05	C
TISP	1	0.32	1.47	0.31	C	0.47	0.10	B	0.83	0.10	C	0.39	0.06	C
TISP	2	0.32	1.22	0.18	C	0.39	0.06	B	0.85	0.15	C	0.33	0.04	C
TISP	3	0.32	1.11	0.23	C	0.35	0.07	B	0.92	0.14	C	0.32	0.04	C
TISP	4	0.32	1.25	0.17	C	0.40	0.06	B	0.71	0.12	C	0.29	0.05	C
TOCA	1	0.34	1.47	0.31	C	0.50	0.10	B	0.83	0.10	C	0.41	0.06	C
TOCA	2	0.34	1.22	0.18	C	0.41	0.06	B	0.85	0.15	C	0.35	0.04	C
TOCA	3	0.34	1.11	0.23	C	0.38	0.08	B	0.92	0.14	C	0.35	0.05	C
TOCA	4	0.34	1.25	0.17	C	0.43	0.06	B	0.71	0.12	C	0.31	0.05	C
TSHE	1	0.42	1.46	0.01	B	0.61	0.01	A	0.82	0.19	C	0.50	0.04	C
TSHE	2	0.42	1.38	0.03	A	0.58	0.01	A	0.95	0.01	A	0.55	0.01	A
TSHE	3	0.42	1.13	0.02	A	0.48	0.01	A	0.80	0.04	A	0.39	0.01	A
TSHE	4	0.42	1.37	0.01	B	0.58	0.00	A	0.80	0.12	C	0.46	0.06	C
TSME	1	0.42	1.47	0.31	C	0.62	0.13	B	0.82	0.19	C	0.51	0.09	C
TSME	2	0.42	1.22	0.18	C	0.51	0.08	B	1.03	0.13	C	0.52	0.05	C
TSME	3	0.42	1.11	0.23	C	0.47	0.10	B	0.95	0.12	C	0.45	0.06	C
TSME	4	0.42	1.25	0.17	C	0.53	0.07	B	0.80	0.12	C	0.42	0.07	C
TSSP	1	0.38	1.47	0.31	C	0.56	0.12	B	0.82	0.19	C	0.46	0.08	C
TSSP	2	0.38	1.22	0.18	C	0.46	0.07	B	1.03	0.13	C	0.47	0.04	C
TSSP	3	0.38	1.11	0.23	C	0.42	0.09	B	0.95	0.12	C	0.40	0.05	C
TSSP	4	0.38	1.25	0.17	C	0.48	0.07	B	0.80	0.12	C	0.38	0.07	C
ULAL	1	0.57	1.47	0.31	C	0.84	0.17	B	0.83	0.10	C	0.70	0.15	C
ULAL	2	0.57	1.22	0.18	C	0.69	0.10	B	0.85	0.15	C	0.59	0.08	C
ULAL	3	0.57	1.11	0.23	C	0.63	0.13	B	0.92	0.14	C	0.58	0.09	C
ULAL	4	0.57	1.25	0.17	C	0.71	0.10	B	0.71	0.12	C	0.51	0.08	C
ULAM	1	0.46	1.47	0.31	C	0.68	0.14	B	0.83	0.10	C	0.56	0.10	C
ULAM	2	0.46	1.22	0.18	C	0.56	0.08	B	0.85	0.15	C	0.48	0.05	C
ULAM	3	0.46	1.11	0.23	C	0.51	0.10	B	0.92	0.14	C	0.47	0.06	C
ULAM	4	0.46	1.25	0.17	C	0.58	0.08	B	0.71	0.12	C	0.41	0.06	C
ULCR	1	0.57	1.47	0.31	C	0.84	0.17	B	0.83	0.10	C	0.70	0.15	C
ULCR	2	0.57	1.22	0.18	C	0.69	0.10	B	0.85	0.15	C	0.59	0.08	C
ULCR	3	0.57	1.11	0.23	C	0.63	0.13	B	0.92	0.14	C	0.58	0.09	C
ULCR	4	0.57	1.25	0.17	C	0.71	0.10	B	0.71	0.12	C	0.51	0.08	C
ULPU	1	0.46	1.47	0.31	C	0.68	0.14	B	0.83	0.10	C	0.56	0.10	C
ULPU	2	0.46	1.22	0.18	C	0.56	0.08	B	0.85	0.15	C	0.48	0.05	C
ULPU	3	0.46	1.11	0.23	C	0.51	0.10	B	0.92	0.14	C	0.47	0.06	C
ULPU	4	0.46	1.25	0.17	C	0.58	0.08	B	0.71	0.12	C	0.41	0.06	C
ULRU	1	0.48	1.47	0.31	C	0.71	0.15	B	0.83	0.10	C	0.59	0.11	C
ULRU	2	0.48	1.22	0.18	C	0.58	0.09	B	0.85	0.15	C	0.49	0.06	C
ULRU	3	0.48	1.11	0.23	C	0.53	0.11	B	0.92	0.14	C	0.49	0.07	C

Species code	Size class	Bole init density	Branch-bole ratio	Uncert B-B ratio	Uncert_bb ratio code	FWD initial density	Uncert FWD density	Uncert FWD code	Relative density	Uncert Rel density	Uncert Rel Den code	Decayed density	Uncert Decayed density	Uncert Decayed code
ULRU	4	0.48	1.25	0.17	C	0.60	0.08	B	0.71	0.12	C	0.43	0.06	C
ULSE	1	0.57	1.47	0.31	C	0.84	0.17	B	0.83	0.10	C	0.70	0.15	C
ULSE	2	0.57	1.22	0.18	C	0.69	0.10	B	0.85	0.15	C	0.59	0.08	C
ULSE	3	0.57	1.11	0.23	C	0.63	0.13	B	0.92	0.14	C	0.58	0.09	C
ULSE	4	0.57	1.25	0.17	C	0.71	0.10	B	0.71	0.12	C	0.51	0.08	C
ULSP	1	0.50	1.47	0.31	C	0.74	0.15	B	0.83	0.10	C	0.61	0.12	C
ULSP	2	0.50	1.22	0.18	C	0.61	0.09	B	0.85	0.15	C	0.52	0.06	C
ULSP	3	0.50	1.11	0.23	C	0.55	0.11	B	0.92	0.14	C	0.50	0.07	C
ULSP	4	0.50	1.25	0.17	C	0.63	0.09	B	0.71	0.12	C	0.45	0.07	C
ULTH	1	0.57	1.47	0.31	C	0.84	0.17	B	0.83	0.10	C	0.70	0.15	C
ULTH	2	0.57	1.22	0.18	C	0.69	0.10	B	0.85	0.15	C	0.59	0.08	C
ULTH	3	0.57	1.11	0.23	C	0.63	0.13	B	0.92	0.14	C	0.58	0.09	C
ULTH	4	0.57	1.25	0.17	C	0.71	0.10	B	0.71	0.12	C	0.51	0.08	C
UMCA	1	0.51	1.47	0.31	C	0.75	0.16	B	0.83	0.10	C	0.62	0.12	C
UMCA	2	0.51	1.22	0.18	C	0.62	0.09	B	0.85	0.15	C	0.53	0.06	C
UMCA	3	0.51	1.11	0.23	C	0.56	0.12	B	0.92	0.14	C	0.51	0.08	C
UMCA	4	0.51	1.25	0.17	C	0.64	0.09	B	0.71	0.12	C	0.46	0.07	C
VAAR	1	0.47	1.47	0.31	C	0.69	0.14	B	0.83	0.10	C	0.57	0.10	C
VAAR	2	0.47	1.22	0.18	C	0.57	0.09	B	0.85	0.15	C	0.49	0.06	C
VAAR	3	0.47	1.11	0.23	C	0.52	0.11	B	0.92	0.14	C	0.48	0.07	C
VAAR	4	0.47	1.25	0.17	C	0.59	0.08	B	0.71	0.12	C	0.42	0.06	C

(Appendix 4 continued on next page)

(Appendix 4 continued)

FWD Absolute and Relative Density Metadata (for Appendix 4)

Fieldname	Definition	Code	Units/explanation
species_code	genus-species code		Refer to Appendices 2 and 3
Size class	size code	1	0-1 cm
	size code	2	1-5 cm
	size code	3	5-12 cm
Bole init density	bole initial density		g/cm³
Branch bole ratio	branch to bole ratio		
uncert_bb ratio	uncertainty of branch to bole ratio		
uncert_bbr_code	uncertainty code for bbr	A	sampled green branch density with standard error
		B	sampled green branch density no standard error
	uncertainty code for bbr	C	unsampled green branch density
FWD_init density	branch initial density		g/cm³
Uncert_init density	uncertainty of initial density		g/cm³
uncert_init density code	uncertainty code for fwd_iden	A	species initial branch density sampled
Uncert FWD init density code	uncertainty code for fwd_iden	B	unsampled green, use BBR to obtain green
Rel density	fwd relative density		Dimensionless
Uncert rel density	uncertainty of fwd relative density		Dimensionless
Uncert rel density code	uncertainty code for relative density	A	decayed density sampled with standard error
		B	decayed density sampled no standard error
		C	decayed density calculated from mean
Decayed density	FWD decayed density		g/cm³
Uncert_decayed den	uncertainty of decayed density		g/cm³
Uncert decay density code	uncertainty code for decayed density	A	species decayed density sampled with standard error
		B	species decayed density sampled no standard error
		C	unsampled decayed

APPENDIX 5.—Examples of estimates of the mean and uncertainty for various levels in the calculation hierarchy (red spruce, *Picea rubens*) on five FIA sample plots in Maine with the assumption that density was not directly measured

Within a Decay or Size Class for a Species and Site

In plot 407074 there is a total of 18.13 m³/ha of decay class 3 CWD. The estimated mean density is 0.316 Mg/m³ and uncertainty in density is 0.112 Mg/m³. The mean mass and the uncertainty are therefore:

$$\text{Mass}_{DC\text{-}Sp\text{-}S} = 18.13 \text{m}^3/\text{ha}*0.316\text{Mg/m}^3 = 5.73 \text{ Mg/ha}$$

$$\text{UncertaintyMass}_{DC\text{-}Sp\text{-}S} = 18.13 \text{m}^3/\text{ha}*0.112\text{Mg/m}^3 = 2.031 \text{ Mg/ha}$$

Within a Species and Site

In plot 407074 there were pieces in decay classes 2-4 and none in decay classes 1 and 5. Because the density of this species was not measured directly, density of all decay classes is likely either underestimated or overestimated to the same degree and we can assume the uncertainties in these decay classes are positively correlated. Therefore, the mean and uncertainty of mass for this plot are:

$$\text{Mass}_{Sp\text{-}S} = 0 \text{ Mg/ha}+0.519 \text{ Mg/ha}+5.73 \text{ Mg/ha}+1.39 \text{ Mg/ha}+0 \text{ Mg/ha}$$
$$= 7.64 \text{ Mg/ha}$$

$$\text{Uncertainty Mass}_{Sp\text{-}S} = 0.07 \text{ Mg/ha}+2.03 \text{ Mg/ha}+0.31 \text{ Mg/ha} = 2.41 \text{ Mg/ha}$$

The relative uncertainty is therefore 31 percent.

Within a Species for All Sites

There are five plots each with its own mass and uncertainty estimate. Assuming density in all plots is underestimated or overestimated to the same degree, the total mass and uncertainty are:

$$\text{Mass}_{Sp} = 7.64 \text{ Mg/ha}+15.15 \text{ Mg/ha}+1.34 \text{ Mg/ha}+1.45 \text{ Mg/ha}+1.42 \text{ Mg/ha}$$
$$= 27.00 \text{ Mg/ha}$$

$$\text{Uncertainty Mass}_{Sp} = 2.41 \text{ Mg/ha}+4.02 \text{ Mg/ha}+0.21 \text{ Mg/ha}+3.76 \text{ Mg/ha}$$
$$+0.35 \text{ Mg/ha} = 10.75 \text{ Mg/ha}$$

The relative uncertainty is therefore 39.8 percent.

(continued on next page)

Within a Site

The uncertainty in mass for a site combines the mass of all the species at a site. Because there is no reason to believe that uncertainty in one species is correlated with another, the mean and uncertainty would be:

$$\text{Mass}_S = 7.64 \text{ Mg/ha} + 5.99 \text{ Mg/ha} = 13.64 \text{ Mg/ha}$$

$$\text{Uncertainty Mass}_S = \text{square root } (2.41^2 + 0.61^2) = 2.49 \text{ Mg/ha}$$

The relative uncertainty is therefore 18 percent.

APPENDIX 6.—Examples of estimates of the mean and uncertainty for various levels in the calculation hierarchy (red spruce, *Picea rubens*) on five FIA sample plots in Maine with the assumption that density was directly measured

Within a Decay or Size Class for a Species and Site

In plot 407074 there is a total of 18.13 m^3/ha of decay class 3 CWD. The estimated mean density is 0.316 Mg/m^3 and uncertainty in density is 0.112 Mg/m^3. The mean mass and the uncertainty are therefore:

$$\text{Mass}_{DC\text{-}Sp\text{-}S} = 18.13 m^3/ha * 0.316 Mg/m^3 = 5.73 \text{ Mg/ha}$$

$$\text{UncertaintyMass}_{DC\text{-}Sp\text{-}S} = 18.13 m^3/ha * 0.112 Mg/m^3 = 2.031 \text{ Mg/ha}$$

Within a Species and Site

In plot 407074 there were pieces in decay classes 2-4 and none in decay classes 1 and 5). Because the density for all decay classes was measured, the uncertainty is related to random sampling error. Therefore, the mean and uncertainty of mass for this plot are:

$$\text{Mass}_{Sp\text{-}S} = 0 \text{ Mg/ha} + 0.519 \text{ Mg/ha} + 5.73 \text{ Mg/ha} + 1.39 \text{ Mg/ha} + 0 \text{ Mg/ha}$$
$$= 7.64 \text{ Mg/ha}$$

$$\text{Uncertainty Mass}_{Sp\text{-}S} = \text{Square root } (0.07^2 + 2.03^2 + 0.31^2) = 2.06 \text{ Mg/ha}$$

The relative uncertainty is therefore 27 percent.

Within a Species for All Sites

There are five plots each with its own mass and uncertainty estimate. There is no reason to believe the uncertainty in the plots is correlated. Therefore, the total mass and uncertainty are:

$$\text{Mass}_{Sp} = 7.64 \text{ Mg/ha} + 15.15 \text{ Mg/ha} + 1.34 \text{ Mg/ha} + 1.45 \text{ Mg/ha} + 1.42 \text{ Mg/ha}$$
$$= 27.00 \text{ Mg/ha}$$

$$\text{Uncertainty Mass}_{Sp} = \text{square root } (2.06^2 + 2.89^2 + 0.13^2 + 0.27^2 + 0.28^2)$$
$$= 3.57 \text{ Mg/ha}$$

The relative uncertainty is therefore 13 percent.

(continued on next page)

Within a Site

The uncertainty in mass for a site combines the mass of all the species at a site. There is no reason to believe that uncertainty in one species is correlated with another. Therefore, the mean and uncertainty would be:

$$\text{Mass}_s = 7.64 \text{ Mg/ha} + 5.99 \text{ Mg/ha} = 13.64 \text{ Mg/ha}$$

$$\text{Uncertainty Mass}_s = \text{square root } (2.06^2 + 0.28^2) = 2.08 \text{ Mg/ha}$$

The relative uncertainty is therefore 15 percent.